The Complete Diabetic Cookbook

Over 2000 Days of Diabetic Delights | Simple, Healthy Recipes for Optimal Blood Sugar Control | Your Ultimate Meal Plan for Diabetic Wellness

Table of Contents

Introduction

Our physical well-being is often neglected in the hectic pace of our modern life. We find ourselves engulfed in a maelstrom of approaching deadlines, familial responsibilities, and the never-ending balancing act that is our everyday responsibilities. Our bodies silently bear the brunt of the weight in the midst of all of this chaos, and for some of us, that burden manifests as diabetes.

Imagine yourself in the center of a bustling coffee shop, with the aroma of freshly brewed coffee filling the air. There are many delectable treats on the menu, and each one is more seductive than the one before it. However, as you review your options, a knot appears in the pit of your stomach. As you calculate the carbohydrates and sugars and consider how they can affect your blood sugar levels, your mind is racing. Every time they indulge in even the most innocent of pleasures, people with diabetes have to negotiate a difficult mental maze.

This is not an isolated incident; millions of people deal with the intricate dance of managing their diabetes on a regular basis. It's a journey that calls for constant observation, close examination of nutritional labels, and a never-ending quest for delicious meals that are also diabetic-friendly. You'll be asking yourself questions like, "What can I eat?" during this journey. How can I manage my health and taste buds at the same time? Is eating something I enjoy doable without endangering my health?

Developed with you in mind, this cookbook is called the "Diabetic Cookbook." You are at the proper spot if you are nodding along or quietly acknowledging the issues. This is more than just a cookbook; it's a travel companion that will help you rediscover your love of cuisine without sacrificing your health.

Acknowledging the obstacles associated with a diabetes diagnosis is the first step towards conquering diabetes. We are all too familiar with these emotions, particularly the dread of the unknown, the frustration that comes with following dietary restrictions, and the anxiety that comes with food shopping. It's more than just a cookbook; for people who are finding it difficult to manage the difficulties associated with diabetes, it's a lifeline.

Why should you read these pages and waste part of your precious time? because you might discover other content here besides recipes. You'll discover yourself in a universe where delectable and foods low in sugar coexist together. You won't have to be concerned about being restricted to monotonous and dull meals ever again; instead, you'll embark on a culinary adventure that celebrates the diverse flavors that the globe has to offer.

This cookbook's brilliance lies not just in its well curated selection of delectable recipes, but also in the increased autonomy it grants its users. Imagine walking into any kitchen with total confidence, knowing that you have all the skills necessary to create foods that satisfy the palate while simultaneously giving the body the nutrition it needs. Since you will now be the conductor of a symphony of tastes that are especially tailored to satisfy the needs of your unique diet, you won't feel like an outsider in the world of cuisine.

You will discover a wealth of information that isn't just for the kitchen as you go through the book. This book offers a comprehensive guide to every aspect of life with diabetes, from navigating social situations with grace to deciphering the complexity of food labels. It's not just about controlling your blood sugar; it's also about regaining control over your life and realizing its full potential.

At this point, you may be questioning who I am to guide you on this path. This is not the place or time for me to brag about you or show off my achievements. I am merely another traveler on this journey, someone who has experienced similar ups and downs, confronted similar fears, and come out on the other side with a deep understanding of what it means to lead a healthy life with diabetes.

My intention in writing these pages is not to teach, but to communicate - to impart the information I have learned from my own experience, the insight I have received from talking to experts, and the collective wisdom of a community that has traveled this route before. Together, we will embark on a journey that will fundamentally transform our lives and turn diabetes into a motivator for living a larger, more active life rather than a barrier.

So, know, my dear reader, that you are not alone in feeling the weight of dietary limitations or the disappointment of meals that did not satisfy them. This is more than just a cookbook; it's an invitation to a taste revolution and a reference that will make you exclaim, "This is the right book for me!" It gives me great joy to welcome you to a world where food is a reason to celebrate as much as a means of survival. Both the "Diabetic Cookbook" and a newfound appreciation for each and every meal are waiting for you.

Understanding Diabetes

Millions of individuals worldwide suffer from diabetes, a chronic medical condition brought on by a complex interplay between lifestyle factors and a person's metabolism, both of which have a significant impact on the person's quality of life. This paper explores the intricacies of diabetes, looking at its different subtypes, underlying causes, risk factors, subtle symptoms, diagnostic procedures that reveal the condition's existence, and—above all—the critical need of managing the disease well.

Types of Diabetes

Diabetes is actually a spectrum of illnesses, each with distinct characteristics, rather than a single sickness. Diabetes is a broad category of illnesses rather than a single condition. Diabetes comes in a number of forms; types 1 and 2 are the most prevalent, but gestational diabetes and other less frequent forms also exist.

An autoimmune condition called Type 1 diabetes is frequently identified in children or adolescents. In this type of diabetes, the body's immune system accidentally attacks and kills the pancreatic beta cells that produce insulin, which raises blood sugar levels. Because of this, people with type 1 diabetes are insulin-dependent and require injections of exogenous insulin to keep their blood sugar levels within normal ranges.

Diabetes Type 2: Adults are typically diagnosed with this form of the disease, which is significantly more prevalent. It is brought on by the body's incapacity to properly use insulin. To offset this resistance, the pancreas initially produces an excessive amount of insulin. After a while, though, the pancreas can no longer maintain normal glucose levels. Along with genes, poor diet, inactivity, and behavior are among the lifestyle factors that have a substantial impact on the development of type 2 diabetes.

Diabetes Only affecting certain women, gestational diabetes is a disorder that only lasts during pregnancy. It's a temporary condition that comes up during pregnancy. Even while it usually goes away after birth, having it increases the risk of developing type 2 diabetes later in life.

Causes and Risk Factors

Diabetes develops as a result of both environmental factors and genetic predisposition. These two categories of risk variables combine to create diabetes. Developing effective preventive strategies requires a thorough understanding of the components that contribute to the issue.

A person's family history of diabetes has a major impact on their risk of having the condition. Individuals with diabetes who have close relatives with the disease are more likely to have the condition themselves. A person's chance of developing diabetes is further increased by a few genetic markers.

Aspects of the Environment: A person's lifestyle choices significantly enhance their risk of having diabetes. Diets high in unhealthy fats and processed sugars raise the risk of type 2 diabetes as well as sedentary lifestyle patterns. Furthermore, it has been proposed that environmental variables, such as exposure to specific chemicals, may have a role in the development of diabetes.

Obesity: One of the biggest risk factors for Type 2 diabetes is believed to be obesity. Keeping a healthy weight is crucial for both the prevention and treatment of diabetes, as insulin resistance is linked to excess adipose tissue, especially in the abdominal area.

Symptoms and Diagnosis

It is essential to identify the symptoms of diabetes in order to start treatment as soon as possible. Among the most common signs of diabetes are increased thirst, increased frequency of urination, inexplicable weight loss, and persistent weariness. Whether a person has type 1 or type 2 diabetes can affect their symptoms.

Diabetes Type 1 Symptoms Individuals with Type 1 diabetes may have significant, sometimes unexpected symptoms. Acute thirst, frequent urination, unexpected weight loss, and increased hunger are some possible signs. Irritation and fatigue are some common adverse effects.

Symptoms of type 2 diabetes include: It is conceivable that type 2 diabetes symptoms will initially manifest slowly and softly. Increased thirst, fatigue, frequent urination, and blurred eyesight are typical symptoms. Many people may not show any symptoms for an extended period of time, which emphasizes the importance of getting tested on a regular basis.

Methods of Diagnosis A combination of blood tests and a clinical examination is needed to diagnose diabetes. Oral glucose tolerance testing, HbA1c testing, and fasting blood sugar testing provide valuable insights into the evolution of blood sugar levels over time. Medical professionals consider the patient's symptoms, medical history, and any possible risk factors during the diagnosing process.

Importance of Managing Diabetes

Diabetes that is not properly managed can have serious repercussions that can negatively impact practically every organ system in the body. It has a wide range of negative effects on health, including nephropathy, neuropathy, cardiovascular problems, and an elevated risk of infections. Effective diabetes management is not an option; rather, it is a must to reduce the effects of these risks and lead a purposeful life.

Diabetes significantly raises the risk of cardiovascular diseases, which is one of the main risk factors for the condition. To avoid heart-related problems, medication must be taken, lifestyle modifications must be made, and regular exams are necessary. High blood pressure, excessive cholesterol, and high blood sugar are some of these consequences.

Insomnia and Diabetes: Long-term high blood sugar exposure can harm the kidneys and cause neuropathy, or damage to the nerves (also known as nephropathy). The management and prevention of these problems depend heavily on lifestyle modifications, consistent medication administration, and close observation.

Preventing Infections People with diabetes have weakened immune systems, which increases their risk of infection. Maintaining vaccination schedules, giving them the proper wound care, and regularly monitoring them can all help prevent infections.

Life Quality: Good diabetes management enhances overall health, which transcends the physical aspects of the disease. Individuals with diabetes can lead fulfilling lives if they prioritize leading a healthy lifestyle, follow their doctor's instructions, and prioritize getting regular checkups.

Acknowledging the complexity of diabetes is a necessary first step toward effective treatment. If people are aware of the different varieties of diabetes, its causes and risk factors, its symptoms, and the significance of early diagnosis, they can take preventative steps toward leading a life free from the limitations imposed by the problems of diabetes. The importance of effectively managing diabetes cannot be overstated; it is not only a medical necessity but also a means to a life full of vitality, wellbeing, and resilience.

Nutritional Fundamentals for Diabetics

Nutrition emerges as a crucial character in the complex dance of controlling diabetes, holding tremendous impact over blood sugar levels and general health and wellbeing. This chapter delves into the nutritional fundamentals that form the bedrock of a lifestyle that is friendly to people living with diabetes. Topics covered include the nuanced relationships between Carbs, proteins, and fats; unraveling the mysteries of the glycemic index and glycemic load; delving into the importance of portion control and meal timing; and providing the reader with the skills necessary to decipher the language used on food labels.

Carbs, Proteins, and Fats

The main topic of discussion when it comes to diabetes nutrition is the role of carbohydrates. The bulk of the diet consists of carbohydrates. Despite the outdated notion that carbohydrates should be avoided at all costs, it is imperative to understand that not all carbohydrates are made equal. Complex carbohydrates are necessary for a well-balanced diet and are present in vegetables, legumes, and whole grains. This helps to avoid sharp spikes in blood sugar levels since they release glucose more gradually. However, due to their quick effect on blood sugar, simple carbohydrates—which are abundant in processed sweets and refined grains—should be consumed with caution.

Proteins: To keep blood glucose levels constant, proteins are a necessary component. Including them in the diet can be very beneficial for diabetics because of their minimal impact on blood glucose levels. Lean protein choices like chicken, fish, tofu, and lentils are the best options if you want to stay energy-rich without experiencing the negative blood-sugar swings associated with high-carb meals.

In the case of fats, the notion that one should drastically limit their intake of fats must be refuted by distinguishing between good and poor fats. Good sources of monounsaturated and polyunsaturated fats that help regulate diabetes are avocados, almonds, and olive oil. These fats improve cardiovascular health and make individuals feel fuller for longer, both of which help with weight control. However, processed and fried meals frequently contain trans and saturated fats, which should both be consumed in moderation as they raise the risk of cardiovascular disease and insulin resistance.

Glycemic Index and Glycemic Load

People can utilize the glycemic index (GI) and glycemic load (GL) as useful tools to assist them sort through the many dietary options that are accessible to them. Through comprehension of these concepts, individuals with diabetes can make informed decisions about how specific foods affect their blood sugar levels.

The Glycemic Index, sometimes known as the GI, is a system of numbers that classifies carbohydrates based on how likely they are to raise blood sugar levels. Meals with a high glycemic index (GI) raise blood sugar levels quickly, while foods with a low GI raise blood sugar levels more gradually. For diabetics, foods having a low glycemic index (GI) are suggested to help them maintain stable blood sugar levels. Examples of these foods include whole grains, legumes, and low-starch vegetables.

Glycemic Load (GL): Unlike the Glycemic Index (GI), which assesses the impact of each specific food item, the GL considers both the kind and amount of carbohydrates consumed. It offers a more comprehensive view of how various meals impact blood sugar levels. For instance, although having a high GI, watermelon has a low GL since a single slice only comprises a little amount of carbohydrates. This is because there is a lot of water in the fruit.

Portion Control and Meal Timing

Regulating the Size of Portion The adage "everything in moderation" is particularly applicable to those trying to control their diabetes. Portion control is a crucial element in lowering blood sugar spikes. Techniques like measuring serving sizes, switching to standard dishes, and resisting the urge to overeat can all be used to promote mindful eating. Properly balancing the quantity of carbohydrates, proteins, and fats in the diet might have a harmonic influence on blood sugar levels.

Because of the rhythm of meals, time is a crucial component in the management of diabetes. Establishing a regular meal schedule helps the body feel regular and supports the maintenance of appropriate blood sugar levels. If one spreads out their meals throughout the day and consumes healthy snacks in between large meals, they can prevent significant fluctuations in their blood sugar levels. Furthermore, the timing of carbohydrate consumption in respect to exercise may change the way the body uses glucose. This emphasizes how important it is to plan meals around regular activities like working out and other hobbies.

Reading Food Labels

For numerous individuals, deciphering the perplexing web of food labels is akin to solving a puzzle. Nonetheless, developing this skill is essential if one wants to base dietary choices on accurate information. Some crucial areas to focus on are the following:

The serving's size: You can prevent inadvertently taking more carbohydrates and other nutrients than necessary by paying attention to the serving size. Be advised that the serving size listed on the package might not match up exactly with the amount you wish to eat.

All of the carbohydrates: All forms of carbohydrates are covered in this section, including sugars and fibers. Pay close attention to the breakdown to determine where the carbohydrates are coming from, and prioritize making complete, unprocessed food choices.

Dietary fiber can help diabetics manage their blood sugar levels, making it a valuable ally. Eat plenty of fruits, vegetables, whole grains, and other foods high in dietary fiber.

Sugars: While not all sugars are bad for you, it's important to know the difference between sugars that are added to food on purpose and those that are naturally present in the food we eat. Better blood sugar regulation is linked to consuming fewer added sugars.

An item's composition can be inferred from its ingredient list, which is provided below. Look for products with minimal processing, easily identified ingredients, and no unnecessary additions.

Gaining an effective toolkit for one's health and wellbeing is similar to understanding the fundamentals of a diabetes diet, which is particularly crucial for those who have the disease. If people with diabetes are aware of the complex interactions between carbohydrates, proteins, and fats; understand the glycemic index and glycemic load; practice attentive meal timing and portion control; and read food labels with confidence, they may confidently traverse the culinary landscape. This chapter is not merely a manual; rather, it is an invitation to take back mastery over one's diet and clear the path to a more balanced, vibrant existence.

Building a Balanced Diabetic Plate

The capacity to prepare nutrient-dense, well-balanced meals is crucial for the effective treatment of diabetes, in addition to specific nutrients. This chapter presents a thorough strategy for feeding the body while controlling blood sugar levels. It explores the Plate Method as a guiding idea, clarifies the nuances of creating balanced meals, and delves into the world of smart snacking.

The Plate Method

People with diabetes can create a plate with a healthy balance of meals more easily by using the Plate Method, a visual meal planning tool. It serves as a useful manual that offers a simple way to distribute nutrients and regulate portion size.

How It Operates: Imagine dividing the food on your plate into three portions: half would go toward starchy-free veggies, one-fourth would go toward low-fat proteins, and the remaining portion would go toward carbohydrates. When it comes to cooking balanced meals that also assist maintain more stable blood sugar levels, this visual representation is useful.

vegetables devoid of starch include: Vegetables devoid of carbohydrates take up the largest section of the platter. These veggies have a broad range of hues and textures that not only provide visual appeal to the meal but also provide vital elements including fiber, vitamins, and minerals. Think about cruciferous veggies like peppers, cauliflower, and broccoli. These veggies are part of a diet that is beneficial to people with diabetes since they have very little effect on blood sugar levels.

Low-Fat Proteins The next quadrant is devoted to low-fat proteins, which are the building blocks of muscle and play a crucial role in the feeling of fullness. Options like as lentils, turkey, salmon, tofu, and chicken offer a multitude of substitutes to suit different nutritional needs and preferences. Proteins are crucial for preserving stable blood sugar levels and preventing the blood sugar rises that often follow meals high in carbohydrates.

Carbs: Taking up the remaining quarter of the plate, carbohydrates are the energy source that needs to be properly monitored. Select whole grains for long-lasting energy that don't spike your blood sugar, such as brown rice, quinoa, or whole wheat pasta. The Plate Method prioritizes the selection of complex carbohydrates above simple sugars, promoting a more nutritious and balanced diet.

Creating Balanced Meals

To prepare meals that are nutritionally sound, a deeper comprehension of food types, portion sizes, and the order in which nutrients should be ingested is needed. Beyond the "Plate

Method," this is the case. This is a how-to for creating meals that are balanced in terms of taste, nutrition, and blood sugar control.

Including a Wide Range of Food Categories: A "balanced meal" is defined as one that includes a number of food categories from which a wide range of nutrients can be consumed. Add some tasty fats to your diet, such avocados or olive oil, along with starch-free vegetables, lean proteins, and complex carbohydrates. You'll feel fuller for longer thanks to this. This combination of nutrients is good for one's overall health and wellbeing.

Sizes of Conscious Portions: Accurately estimating portion sizes is still vital, even with the Plate Method providing visual guidance. A portion of protein is roughly the same size as a regular deck of playing cards, whereas a meal of carbs is around the same size as a tennis ball. A customized meal plan can be made by varying the amount of food eaten at each meal based on personal factors like age, activity level, and metabolic rate.

Sustaining a Proper Macronutrient Balance Maintaining a balanced macronutrient ratio is one of the most crucial parts of meal planning for blood sugar regulation. This involves keeping the proportions of lipids, carbohydrates, and proteins in check. A harmonious distribution of vital nutrients is what you should aim for in order to avoid the harmful effects of an unbalanced diet. For instance, combining a complex carbohydrate with lean protein will reduce the rate at which the body absorbs glucose, hence reducing sudden spikes in blood sugar.

One of the most crucial things to think about while attempting to regulate your blood sugar levels is timing your meals. Regular spacing of meals throughout the day reduces the risk of hypoglycemia and excessive postprandial increases. The risk of hypoglycemia increases with extended fasting. Additionally, the body has easy access to a source of energy when it eats a well-balanced meal before engaging in physical activity.

Smart Snacking

When consumed in moderation and with awareness, snacks can help manage diabetes in addition to being a fun way to consume food. Choosing foods high in nutrients and fiber will help you feel content for longer and prevent sharp fluctuations in blood sugar. This is what it means to snack sensibly.

How to Choose Nutrient-Dense Snacks: Make decisions that will provide you a nutritional boost instead of reaching for snacks that are merely empty calories. Healthy snacks that satisfy your hunger and supply essential nutrients are things like Greek yogurt with berries on top, almonds in a handful, or hashed veggies with hummus.

Selecting the Appropriate Time for Snack Eating: When it comes to deciding whether or not you are snacking, when you eat matters just as much as what you eat. By having a snack in between meals, one can avoid becoming overly hungry and reduce their chance of overindulging during their main meals. Furthermore, consuming a carbohydrate together with a protein or a healthy fat at the same meal can help to keep blood sugar levels steady.

Observing the Indications of Appetite: By being aware of the bodily cues that suggest hunger and making the decision to consume snacks only when one is genuinely hungry rather than out of habit or boredom, one can cultivate a positive relationship with food. Eating thoughtfully encompasses not only the three primary meals of the day but also each and every snack. This makes it possible to guarantee that every single bite is the outcome of a conscious choice.

Meal planning for people with diabetes is a skill that calls for a keen understanding of one's own nutritional needs along with a combination of scientific information and creative thought. The Plate Method provides a practical framework for meal planning, and the concepts of balanced eating and strategic snacking offer a complex method for providing the body with the nourishment it needs. This chapter is not just a manual; rather, it's a call to confidently explore the world of food and to value every meal as a step toward better health and diabetes management.

Essential Kitchen Tools and Ingredients

The kitchen is a more practical aspect of the house where the pursuit of effective diabetes treatment extends beyond the realm of diet theory. This chapter delves into the world of essential kitchen tools and products designed specifically for people managing the complications of diabetes. This investigation serves as a guide for converting the kitchen into a sanctuary of empowered cooking. This exploration is a road plan for turning the kitchen into a haven, from filling the pantry with diabetic-friendly essentials to learning health-conscious cooking methods and obtaining essential kitchen gear.

Diabetic-Friendly Pantry Staples

The pantry alternatives should be carefully considered when building a kitchen that is suited for diabetes. The goal is to put together a group of ingredients that, in addition to improving flavor, also fit the target nutritional profile. Let's examine the basic pantry staples that are appropriate for diabetes and form the foundation of wholesome, nutritionally balanced meals.

Whole Grains: Processed grains have to be avoided in favor of whole grains like quinoa, brown rice, and oats. Due to their lower glycemic index, these grains offer sustained energy instead of the quick bursts that are connected to the refined varieties of these grains.

Legumes include beans, lentils, and chickpeas. Because of their high fiber and protein content, diabetics should always keep these foods in their pantries. They contribute to a feeling of fullness and help keep blood sugar levels consistent.

Nuts and Seeds: Almonds, walnuts, chia seeds, and flaxseeds are among the high-nutrient nuts and seeds. You can find these in the pantry. They have a delicious crunch, but they are also good for you because they are full of fiber, essential minerals, and healthy fats.

Healthy Oils: Olive and avocado oils are among the healthier options for your heart. A significant portion of these oils are made up of monounsaturated fats, which are good for the heart and have no effect on blood sugar levels.

Vinegars: There is some evidence to suggest that vinegars, especially apple cider vinegar, may assist manage diabetes. Many studies have demonstrated the potential benefits of vinegar consumption with meals, including reduced blood sugar and increased insulin sensitivity.

Materials from Aromatic Plants: Increase food flavor without adding too much salt or sugar. Adding distinctive flavors to meals can be achieved by using herbs and spices that don't cause blood sugar fluctuations, like thyme, basil, and cilantro, as well as spices like cinnamon and turmeric.

Alternatives to Sugar: Natural sugar substitutes that can be used to sweeten food without raising blood sugar levels include erythritol, stevia, and monk fruit. These substitutes provide a touch of sweetness without the metabolic consequences associated with regular sugars.

Cooking Techniques for Diabetes

Cooking is more than just a way to prepare food; it's a kind of culinary alchemy that transforms ingredients into nutrient-dense final goods. For those managing their diabetes, it is critical to use cooking techniques that enhance the food's flavor while preserving its nutritional content.

Cooking Techniques That Build Flavor Without Using Too Much Fat Two cooking techniques that improve flavors without using a lot of fat are grilling and roasting. These techniques reduce the need for extra oils while adding a delicious smokiness to whatever food you're cooking, including fruits, vegetables, and lean meats.

Steaming: Vegetables can be prepared quickly and still retain their natural nutrients and vibrancy when cooked gently, like steaming. This is an extremely helpful way for those who wish to add taste to their food without sacrificing any of its nutritional value.

Sautéing: If you use only a standard amount of oil when sautéing, you may quickly cook vegetables and proteins without sacrificing their nutritional content or unique texture. By employing this method, food is given additional depth without needlessly adding fat.

Cooking at a Low Heat For individuals who are overly busy, the slow cooker has become an invaluable tool. It allows you to prepare delicious and nourishing meals with the least amount of effort. Furthermore, flavors can meld together with lengthy cooking without needing an excessive quantity of added sweets or fats.

Cooking in Groups: Cooking in batches is a concept you should adopt if you want to streamline the process of making meals. People who have diabetes may make certain that they have access to options that are both handy and nutritious by creating higher quantities of necessary items and then freezing portions for later use. They will become less reliant on processed or harmful substitutes as a result.

Must-Have Kitchen Tools

The amount of productivity in a kitchen is often determined by the appliances that are accessible for usage. Those who are taking care of their diabetes will discover that having the right tools not only makes cooking easier but also contributes to the creation of healthier meals.

For diabetics, a digital kitchen scale is an indispensable tool because proper portion control is critical to their health. When utilizing a digital kitchen scale, people can more effectively manage their carbohydrate intake and maintain appropriate blood sugar levels since it ensures accurate measurements.

The Finest Quality Knives: Meal prep is made easier and faster when you have a high-quality and sharp knife set. A clean knife set is essential for cooking because it can be used for everything from chopping vegetables to portioning out meats.

Cookware That Allows Food to Be Released Without Oil Using cookware that releases food without the need for oil encourages the preparation of meals with an emphasis on health. Because non-stick pans are easy to clean and do not stick to food, they are ideal for grilling or sautéing with minimal added oil.

A vegetable spiralizer might be a game-changer for people searching for innovative ways to incorporate more vegetables into their diet. Spiralizing vegetables is a creative and enjoyable approach to get more nutrients into your diet. It transforms vegetables like carrots and zucchini into noodles-like strands, offering a nutritious substitute for regular pasta.

Food processor or blender: Among the most versatile kitchen tools are blenders and food processors, which may be used to create sauces, purees, and smoothies. For people who wish to incorporate a range of tastes and textures into their diet, they are incredibly beneficial.

Instant-Read Thermometer: When preparing proteins in particular, it's important to precisely gauge the temperature at which food should be prepared. With the use of an instant-read thermometer, meats can be cooked to ideal temperature without running the risk of being overdone or underdone.

Slow Cooker: Using a slow cooker can be helpful for people who need to control their diabetes but are stressed for time. It allows you to prepare filling, nutrient-dense meals with comparatively little work on your side.

Making a kitchen a safe refuge for diabetics means getting the necessary equipment and culinary techniques, as well as filling the pantry with wholesome foods, in accordance with the person's desired degree of health. This chapter is not merely a manual; rather, it's an invitation to embark on a culinary journey where every instrument and ingredient serves as a paintbrush, creating a canvas of mouthwatering and nourishing dishes. By developing a lively and sustainable approach to meal preparation that is both beneficial to the body and aesthetically beautiful, people with diabetes may take charge of their diabetes care. All they require are the right culinary methods, kitchen gear, and pantry essentials.

Sweeteners and Substitutes

Having a thorough awareness of the different sweeteners and substitutes that are available is crucial to creating a culinary experience that is safe for diabetes. This chapter demystifies the intricacies of sweeteners by analyzing natural alternatives to sugar, delving into the world of artificial sweeteners, and presenting baking guidance that is specifically directed at those who are managing their diabetes.

Healthy Alternatives to Sugar

It's not always necessary to give up one's health in order to achieve sweetness. Indulging in naturally occurring, high-nutrient alternatives to sugar not only satisfies the urge for something sweet but also provides a positive contribution to one's overall health.

The leaves of the Stevia rebaudiana plant are used to make stevia, a natural sweetener. While stevia is sweetened, it doesn't have the same calories or carbs as other sweeteners. Because of its intense sweetness, stevia has become more and more popular as a viable option for people trying to cut back on their sugar intake.

Monk Fruit Condiment: This sweetener is well-known for coming from nature and having no calories. The source from which it is taken is monk fruit. Monk fruit sweetener is a tempting option for diabetics attempting to control their blood sugar levels since it provides sweetness without having the same metabolic impact as sugar.

A sugar alcohol called erythritol adds sweetness without influencing the quantity of sugar taken into the blood. Both in its produced form, which is available for purchase, and in its natural form, which can be found in some fruits. Since erythritol has little influence on glycemic response, it is often used in place of sugar in a wide range of culinary preparations.

Another type of sugar alcohol that can be made from maize or birch wood is called xylitol. Its sweet flavor can be enjoyed without consuming as many calories as sugar, and its impact on blood glucose levels is minimal. Two of the most common uses of xylitol as a sugar substitute are in baking and cooking.

Coconut Sugar: Because of its lower glycemic index, coconut sugar—while still classified as sugar—is thought to be a healthier option than regular white sugar. It's a slightly healthier option to take into consideration because it contains antioxidants and trace amounts of minerals like iron and zinc.

Artificial Sweeteners

Artificial sweeteners are one of the many sugar substitutes available; in spite of their controversy, they do have a place. These potent sweeteners are routinely utilized so that sweetness can be supplied without the glycemic and caloric effects that are associated with sugar.

Aspartame: About 200 times sweeter than sucrose, aspartame is a low-calorie sweetener. Diet soft drinks and sugar-free products are the most common places to find it. Due to its heat sensitivity, it should not be used for high-temperature cooking but can be used for cool drinks and as a tabletop sweetener.

Saccharin: One of the most popular artificial sweeteners in the market for a long time is saccharin. It possesses a sweetness that is roughly 300–400 times greater than sugar and has no calories. Saccharin is a food additive that can be used in baking and other culinary applications because it doesn't break down when heated.

About 600 times sweeter than sugar is sucralose, an artificial sweetener. Sucralose comes from sucrose, from whence it is formed. It can be used in the oven and in the kitchen since it doesn't break down in high temperatures. Many sugar-free products usually employ sucralose as a substitute sweetener.

Stevia or Steviol Glycosides Rebaudioside A: While stevia naturally sweetens food, some steviol glycosides can be processed to make high-adrenaline sweeteners. Rebaudioside A is one instance of this. For example, rebaudioside A is a common sugar substitute used in a wide range of meals and food products.

Baking Tips for Diabetics

For people who are managing their diabetes, baking presents a unique set of challenges due to its particular measurements and chemistry. Yet, if one has the right knowledge and abilities, they can indulge in baking's delights without compromising their attempts to lead a healthy lifestyle.

Made With Whole Grains Flours Try using whole-grain substitutes like coconut flour, almond flour, or whole wheat flour in place of refined flours. These substitutes have more fiber, which contributes to a slower rate of glucose absorption by the body.

Sweeteners of Natural Origin: Try using erythritol, stevia, or monk fruit sweetener as natural sweeteners for your baked goods. Since some components can occasionally be sweeter than sugar and need adjusting the quantity used, it is vital to be aware of the sweetness intensity of these additives.

Cut Down on the Added Fats: While fats are essential for baked products' flavor and texture, it's vital to use moderation when adding them. Consider using healthier fats, such avocado or olive oil, and make an effort to reduce the overall quantity of added fat in the foods you prepare.

Add Nuts and Seeds: Adding nuts and seeds to baked goods is a fantastic method to increase the nutrient content of the final product. They contribute essential nutrients and healthy fats to the meal in addition to enhancing its flavor and texture.

Moderate consumption of baked goods is possible as long as portion sizes are kept under control. To limit your intake of Carbs and prevent consuming too many calories, pay attention to portion sizes. You should portion baked items ahead of time to avoid overindulging.

Consider Using Natural Fruit Purees in Place of Some of the Sugar and Fat in Recipes You could try using natural fruit purees in recipes in place of some of the sugar and fat. A dish can benefit from the addition of pumpkin puree, mashed bananas, or apple sauce to achieve sweetness and moisture without adding more sugar or fat.

When building a kitchen that is suited for diabetics, one of the most crucial procedures is to study alternative sweeteners and substitutes. Those managing their diabetes have a wide range of options when it comes to satisfying their sweet craving, whether they opt for artificial sweeteners or natural alternatives like stevia and monk fruit sweetener. With the right techniques and component substitutions, baking—which is commonly thought of as a culinary challenge for people with diabetes—can become a pleasurable undertaking. This chapter is designed to offer not just as a guide but also as an invitation to explore the vast and tasty world of sweeteners and alternatives. By doing this, readers will be able to create a culinary experience that enhances their love of food and is consistent with their health objectives.

Breakfast Recipes

1. Quinoa and Vegetable Breakfast Dish

- Time Required : 10 mins
- Curing time: 15 mins
- Serves: 2

Ingredients:

- 185g quinoa, rinsed
- 500ml vegetable broth
- 15ml olive oil
- 1 onion, hashed
- 2 bell peppers, hashed
- 1 zucchini, hashed
- 5g smoked paprika
- Salt and pepper to taste
- Fresh herbs

Directions:

1. The vegetable broth should be brought to a boil in a saucepan. When the quinoa is cooked, add it, lower the heat, cover it, and simmer it for 15 minutes.
2. In a separate pan, heat olive oil. Saute the hashed onion until it becomes transparent.
3. When the veggies are soft, add the bell peppers and zucchini to the pan and sauté them.
4. Add the smoked paprika, cooked quinoa, salt, and pepper and stir. Cook for two to three more minutes.
5. Garnish the quinoa and veggie mixture with fresh herbs and serve.

Nutrition Information: Kcals: 350, Protein: 10g, Fat: 8g, Carbs: 60g, Sugar: 5g, Fiber: 8g, Sodium: 800mg

2. Avocado and Egg Breakfast Wrap

- Time Required : 8 mins
- Curing time: 5 mins
- Serves: 1

Ingredients:

- 1 whole-grain wrap
- 1 ripe avocado, hashed
- 2 eggs
- Salt and pepper to taste
- Fresh herbs

Directions:

1. Place a nonstick pan over a medium heat source.
2. To reheat, place the wrap in the pan.
3. Cook the eggs in a different pan until they are scrambled, fried, or poached to your preference.
4. After spreading the hashed avocado onto the warm wrap, add salt, pepper, fried eggs, and fresh herbs on top.
5. After folding, serve the wrap right away.

Nutrition Information: Kcals: 420, Protein: 20g, Fat: 28g, Carbs: 30g, Sugar: 1g, Fiber: 12g, Sodium: 400mg

3. Greek Yogurt and Berry Smoothie

- Time Required : 5 mins
- Curing time: 0 mins
- Serves: 2

Ingredients:

- 240g Greek yogurt
- 150g mixed berries strawberries, blueberries, raspberries
- 1 banana
- 15ml honey
- 240ml almond milk
- Ice cubes optional

Directions:

1. Blend together Greek yogurt, almond milk, honey, banana, and mixed berries in a blender.
2. Process till smooth. If desired, add some ice cubes.
3. Transfer into glasses and serve right away.

Nutrition Information:

Kcals: 250, Protein: 15g, Fat: 5g, Carbs: 40g, Sugar: 25g, Fiber: 6g, Sodium: 100mg

4. Berry and Yogurt Parfait

- Time Required : 7 mins
- Curing time: 0 mins
- Serves: 2

Ingredients:

- 240g Greek yogurt
- 150g mixed berries
- 40g granola
- 15ml honey
- Fresh mint

Directions:

1. Arrange granola, mixed berries, and Greek yogurt in serving glasses.
2. Garnish with fresh mint and drizzle honey over the top.
3. Go through the layers again.
4. Present right away.

Nutrition Information: Kcals: 320, Protein: 15g, Fat: 8g, Carbs: 45g, Sugar: 20g, Fiber: 7g, Sodium: 80mg

5. Roasted Vegetable Frittata

- Time Required : 15 mins
- Curing time: 25 mins
- Serves: 4

Ingredients:

- 6 eggs
- 120ml milk
- 150g cherry tomatoes, halved
- 150g zucchini, hashed
- 150g bell peppers, hashed
- 150g spinach
- 60g feta cheese, crumbled
- Salt and pepper to taste

Directions:

1. Turn the oven on to 180°C.
2. Combine milk and eggs in a bowl. Add pepper and salt for seasoning.
3. Bell peppers, cherry tomatoes, and zucchini should all be sautéed in an ovenproof skillet until they start to soften.
4. Let the spinach wilt in the pan after adding it.
5. Cover the veggies with the egg mixture, top with feta cheese, and place the pan in the oven.
6. Bake the frittata for 20 to 25 minutes, or until it sets and begins to turn golden.
7. Cut into pieces and present.

Nutrition Information: Kcals: 220, Protein: 15g, Fat: 15g, Carbs: 10g, Sugar: 5g, Fiber: 3g, Sodium: 300mg

6. Greek Yogurt and Berry Popsicles

- Time Required : 10 mins
- Freeze Time: 4 hours
- Serves: 6

Ingredients:

- 480g Greek yogurt
- 150g mixed berries strawberries, blueberries, raspberries
- 30ml honey

Directions:

1. Blend honey and Greek yogurt in a plate until thoroughly blended.
2. Fold in mixed berries gently.
3. Fill popsicle molds with mixture using a spoon.
4. Place the popsicle sticks in and freeze until solid, about 4 hours.
5. Before serving, run molds under warm water to release popsicles.

Nutrition Information: Kcals: 120, Protein: 8g, Fat: 3g, Carbs: 15g, Sugar: 12g, Fiber: 2g, Sodium: 40mg

7. Sweet Potato and Kale Hash

- Time Required : 12 mins
- Curing time: 20 mins
- Serves: 3

Ingredients:

- 2 sweet potatoes, peeled and hashed
- 15ml olive oil
- 1 onion, hashed
- 60g kale, hashed
- 5g smoked paprika
- Salt and pepper to taste
- Poached eggs for serving optional

Directions:

1. Hashed sweet potatoes should be boiled until just soft. After draining, set away.
2. Heat the olive oil in a pan. Hashed onion should be sautéed until transparent.
3. Hashed kale and boiling sweet potatoes should be added to the pan.
4. Add salt, pepper, and smoked paprika for seasoning. Sauté the kale until it wilts.
5. Serve on its own or alongside poached eggs.

Nutrition Information: Kcals: 180, Protein: 4g, Fat: 5g, Carbs: 30g, Sugar: 8g, Fiber: 5g, Sodium: 150mg

8. Tomato and Basil Zoodle Salad

- Time Required : 10 mins
- Curing time: 0 mins
- Serves: 2

Ingredients:

- 2 zucchinis, spiralized into zoodles
- 150g cherry tomatoes, halved
- 60ml balsamic vinegar
- 30ml olive oil
- Fresh basil leaves
- Salt and pepper to taste
- Feta cheese optional

Directions:

1. Combine cherry tomatoes and zoodles in a bowl.
2. Whisk together olive oil and balsamic vinegar in a separate dish.
3. Over the zoodle mixture, drizzle the dressing. Toss to coat thoroughly.
4. Add freshly torn basil leaves to the salad. Add pepper and salt for seasoning.
5. If preferred, add some feta cheese as a garnish and serve.

Nutrition Information: Kcals: 160, Protein: 4g, Fat: 12g, Carbs: 12g, Sugar: 8g, Fiber: 3g, Sodium: 100mg

9. Berry Chia Seed Pudding

- Time Required : 5 mins
- Chill Time: 4 hours
- Serves: 2

Ingredients:

- 90g chia seeds
- 360ml almond milk
- 15ml honey
- 5ml vanilla extract
- 150g mixed berries

Directions:

1. Combine the almond milk, honey, vanilla essence, and chia seeds in a plate.
2. After giving it a good stir, cover and chill for four hours or overnight so the chia seeds can absorb the liquid.
3. Before serving, give the pudding a good stir.
4. After adding a layer of mixed berries, serve.

Nutrition Information: Kcals: 220, Protein: 6g, Fat: 12g, Carbs: 25g, Sugar: 10g, Fiber: 12g, Sodium: 80mg

10. Dark Chocolate and Berry Smoothie Dish

- Time Required : 7 mins
- Curing time: 0 mins
- Serves: 1

Ingredients:

- 240ml almond milk
- 150g mixed berries strawberries, blueberries, raspberries
- 1 banana
- 15g dark cocoa powder
- 15g chia seeds
- Toppings: hashed strawberries, dark chocolate chunks, and granola

Directions:

1. Blend together almond milk, banana, dark chocolate powder, mixed berries, and chia seeds in a blender.
2. Process till smooth. If necessary, adjust the thickness by adding more almond milk.
3. Transfer the smoothie onto a plate.
4. Top with hashed strawberries, dark chocolate bits, and granola.
5. Snackle up with a spoon and enjoy!

Nutrition Information: Kcals: 380, Protein: 8g, Fat: 15g, Carbs: 60g, Sugar: 25g, Fiber: 12g, Sodium: 120mg

11. Quinoa and Vegetable Breakfast Dish

- Time Required : 15 mins
- Curing time: 15 mins
- Serves: 2

Ingredients:

- 185g quinoa, cooked
- 15ml olive oil
- 1 bell pepper, hashed
- 1 zucchini, hashed
- 150g cherry tomatoes, halved
- 2 eggs, poached
- Salt and pepper to taste
- Fresh parsley

Directions:

- Heat the olive oil in a skillet over a medium heat.
- Add zucchini and hashed bell peppers. Sauté the veggies till they get soft.
- Add the cherry tomatoes and cooked quinoa and stir. Cook for two to three more minutes.
- Spoon the veggie mixture and quinoa into individual bowls.
- Place a poached egg on top of each dish.
- Add pepper and salt for seasoning.
- Before serving, garnish with fresh parsley.

Nutrition Information: Kcals: 320, Protein: 15g, Fat: 15g, Carbs: 35g, Sugar: 5g, Fiber: 7g, Sodium: 150mg

12.   Avocado and Egg Breakfast Wrap

- Time Required : 10 mins
- Curing time: 5 mins
- Serves: 2

Ingredients:

- 2 whole-grain wraps
- 1 avocado, hashed
- 4 eggs, scrambled
- 75g cherry tomatoes, hashed
- 30ml salsa
- Salt and pepper to taste

Directions:

1. The whole-grain wraps can be microwaved or cooked in a dry skillet.
2. Spoon the scrambled eggs, hashed avocado, and hashed cherry tomatoes among the wrappers.
3. Pour salsa over it.
4. Add pepper and salt for seasoning.
5. After folding, serve the wraps.

Nutrition Information: Kcals: 350, Protein: 15g, Fat: 20g, Carbs: 30g, Sugar: 5g, Fiber: 8g, Sodium: 300mg

13.   Roasted Vegetable Frittata

- Time Required : 15 mins
- Curing time: 25 mins
- Serves: 4

Ingredients:

- 8 huge eggs
- 120ml milk
- 150g cherry tomatoes, halved
- 1 zucchini, hashed
- 1 bell pepper, hashed
- 120g spinach, hashed
- 50g feta cheese, crumbled
- Salt and pepper to taste
- Fresh herbs

Directions:

1. Preheat oven to 180°C.
2. Whisk the eggs and milk together in a plate.
3. Tenderize the veggies by sautéing them in an oven-safe skillet with cherry tomatoes, zucchini, bell pepper, and spinach.
4. Over the veggies in the skillet, pour the egg mixture.
5. Top with feta cheese crumbles.
6. Add pepper and salt for seasoning.
7. Bake the frittata for 20 to 25 minutes, or until it sets.
8. Before serving, add a fresh herb garnish.

Nutrition Information: Kcals: 280, Protein: 18g, Fat: 18g, Carbs: 12g, Sugar: 5g, Fiber: 3g, Sodium: 350mg

Lunch Recipes

14. Grilled Chicken Salad with Lemon Vinaigrette

- Time Required : 15 mins
- Curing time: 15 mins
- Serves: 2

Ingredients:

- 300g chicken breast, grilled and hashed
- 180g mixed salad greens
- 150g cherry tomatoes, halved
- 1 cucumber, hashed
- 60ml feta cheese, crumbled
- 60ml black olives, hashed
- Lemon Vinaigrette: 45ml olive oil, 15ml lemon juice, salt, and pepper to taste

Directions:

1. Toss salad greens, cherry tomatoes, cucumber, feta cheese, and olives in a large platter.
2. Add a hashed and grilled chicken breast on top.
3. To make the vinaigrette, combine the olive oil, lemon juice, salt, and pepper in a standard dish.
4. Pour the vinaigrette onto the salad and give it a little stir.
5. Serve right away.

Nutrition Information: Kcals: 450, Protein: 35g, Fat: 25g, Carbs: 20g, Sugar: 8g, Fiber: 6g, Sodium: 600mg

15. Zucchini Noodles with Pesto and Cherry Tomatoes

- Time Required : 10 mins
- Curing time: 5 mins
- Serves: 2

Ingredients:

- 2 huge zucchinis, spiralized into noodles
- 150g cherry tomatoes, halved
- 60g pesto sauce
- 30g pine nuts, toasted
- Fresh basil leaves

Directions:

1. Sauté zucchini noodles until they are slightly soft in a pan.
2. Add the cherry tomatoes and fully cook.
3. Add pesto sauce and stir until well combined.
4. Transfer to serving plates, top with toasted pine nuts and fresh basil.
5. Serve right away.

Nutrition Information: Kcals: 320, Protein: 8g, Fat: 25g, Carbs: 18g, Sugar: 8g, Fiber: 5g, Sodium: 300mg

16. Lentil and Vegetable Soup

- Time Required : 15 mins
- Curing time: 30 mins
- Serves: 4

Ingredients:
- 200g dried green lentils, rinsed
- 1 onion, hashed
- 2 carrots, hashed
- 2 celery stalks, hashed
- 3 cloves garlic, hashed
- 1 can 400g hashed tomatoes
- 1.5 liters vegetable broth
- 5g cumin
- 5g smoked paprika
- Salt and pepper to taste
- Fresh parsley

Directions:
1. Add the onions, carrots, celery, and garlic to a large pot and sauté until softened.
2. Stir in lentils, smoked paprika, cumin, hashed tomatoes, and vegetable broth. Season with salt and pepper.
3. Once the lentils are soft, bring to a boil, lower the heat, and simmer for 25 to 30 minutes.
4. Modify the seasoning as needed.
5. Serve with fresh parsley as a garnish.

Nutrition Information: Kcals: 280, Protein: 15g, Fat: 1g, Carbs: 50g, Sugar: 8g, Fiber: 18g, Sodium: 900mg

17. Cauliflower Crust Pizza with Vegetables

- Time Required : 20 mins
- Curing time: 25 mins
- Serves: 2

Ingredients:

- 1 medium cauliflower, riced
- 1 egg
- 60g mozzarella cheese, shredded
- 30g Parmesan cheese, grated
- 2g dried oregano
- 2g garlic powder
- Salt and pepper to taste
- 120ml tomato sauce
- 150g mixed vegetables bell peppers, cherry tomatoes, spinach
- 30g feta cheese, crumbled
- Fresh basil

Directions:

1. Preheat oven to 200°C.
2. Riced cauliflower, egg, Parmesan, mozzarella, oregano, garlic powder, salt, and pepper should all be combined in a plate.
3. To create a crust, press the mixture into a flat pan lined with parchment paper.
4. Bake for 15-20 minutes, or until the crust sets and turns brown.
5. Cover the crust with tomato sauce, then sprinkle feta cheese and mixed vegetables over top.
6. Bake for ten to fifteen more minutes.
7. Garnish with fresh basil before serving.

Nutrition Information: Kcals: 320, Protein: 20g, Fat: 18g, Carbs: 25g, Sugar: 8g, Fiber: 8g, Sodium: 800mg

18. Turkey and Quinoa Stuffed Peppers

- Time Required : 20 mins
- Curing time: 30 mins
- Serves: 4

Ingredients:
- 4 huge bell peppers, halved and seeds removed
- 185g quinoa, cooked
- 500g ground turkey
- 1 onion, hashed
- 2 cloves garlic, hashed
- 1 can 400g black beans, drained and rinsed
- 150g corn kernels
- 5g cumin
- 5g chili powder
- Salt and pepper to taste
- 240ml tomato sauce
- 120g cheddar cheese, shredded
- Fresh cilantro

Directions:
1. Preheat oven to 180°C.
2. Cook ground turkey, onion, and garlic in a pan until the turkey is done.
3. Add the black beans, corn, cumin, chili powder, cooked quinoa, salt, and pepper.
4. Spoon mixture into bell pepper halves.
5. Cover the filled peppers with tomato sauce and top with cheddar cheese.
6. Bake for 25–30 minutes, or until the cheese is bubbling and melted.
7. Before serving, garnish with fresh cilantro.

Nutrition Information: Kcals: 420, Protein: 35g, Fat: 15g, Carbs: 40g, Sugar: 8g, Fiber: 10g, Sodium: 600mg

19. Chickpea and Spinach Curry

- Time Required : 10 mins
- Curing time: 25 mins
- Serves: 4

Ingredients:
- 30ml olive oil
- 1 onion, finely hashed
- 3 cloves garlic, hashed
- 15g ginger, grated
- 20g curry powder
- 1 can 400g chickpeas, drained and rinsed
- 1 can 400ml coconut milk
- 30g baby spinach
- Salt and pepper to taste
- Fresh cilantro

Directions:
1. Heat the olive oil in a large pan. Fry the ginger, garlic, and onion until aromatic.
2. Stir in curry powder for one to two minutes.
3. Stir in the coconut milk and chickpeas. Simmer for 15-20 minutes.
4. Add baby spinach and stir until it wilts.
5. Add pepper and salt for seasoning. Garnish with fresh cilantro.
6. Serve over quinoa or brown rice.

Nutrition Information: Kcals: 380, Protein: 10g, Fat: 25g, Carbs: 30g, Sugar: 5g, Fiber: 8g, Sodium: 700mg

20. Shrimp and Asparagus Stir-Fry

- Time Required : 15 mins
- Curing time: 10 mins
- Serves: 2

Ingredients:
- 200g shrimp, peeled and deveined
- 1 bunch asparagus, trimmed and cut into 2-inch pieces
- 30ml soy sauce
- 15ml oyster sauce
- 15ml sesame oil
- 15ml rice vinegar
- 15ml hoisin sauce
- 15ml olive oil
- 2 cloves garlic, hashed
- 5g ginger, grated
- Sesame seeds

Directions:
1. Combine the soy sauce, hoisin sauce, sesame oil, oyster sauce, and rice vinegar on a plate.
2. In a large pan or wok, heat the olive oil. Add the ginger and garlic.
3. Stir-fry the prawns until they turn pink.
4. Stir-fry the asparagus until it becomes crisp-tender by adding more.
5. Pour the sauce over the shrimp and asparagus. Toss to coat thoroughly.
6. Garnish with sesame seeds before serving.

Nutrition Information: Kcals: 320, Protein: 25g, Fat: 18g, Carbs: 15g, Sugar: 5g, Fiber: 5g, Sodium: 1200mg

21. Greek Chicken Souvlaki Skewers

- Time Required : 15 mins
- Curing time: 15 mins
- Serves: 4

Ingredients:
- 500g chicken breast, cut into cubes
- 60ml olive oil
- 30ml lemon juice
- 5g dried oregano
- 2 cloves garlic, hashed
- Salt and pepper to taste
- Cherry tomatoes and red onion for skewering
- Tzatziki sauce for serving

Directions:
1. Combine the olive oil, lemon juice, garlic, dried oregano, salt, and pepper in a plate.
2. For at least fifteen minutes, marinate the chicken cubes in the marinade.
3. Cherry tomatoes, red onion, and marinated chicken are threaded onto skewers.
4. Grill the chicken for ten to fifteen minutes on each skewer.
5. Add tzatziki sauce and serve.Combine the olive oil, lemon juice, garlic, dried oregano, salt, and pepper in a plate.
6. For at least fifteen minutes, marinate the chicken cubes in the marinade.
7. Cherry tomatoes, red onion, and marinated chicken are threaded onto skewers.
8. Grill the chicken for ten to fifteen minutes on each skewer.
9. Add tzatziki sauce and serve.

Nutrition Information: Kcals: 280, Protein: 25g, Fat: 18g, Carbs: 5g, Sugar: 2g, Fiber: 1g, Sodium: 400mg

22. Cucumber and Tuna Salad

- Time Required : 10 mins
- Curing time: 0 mins
- Serves: 2

Ingredients:
- 2 cucumbers, thinly hashed
- 2 cans 200g each tuna, drained
- 60g red onion, thinly hashed
- 30g Kalamata olives, hashed
- 60ml olive oil
- 30ml red wine vinegar
- 5g dried oregano
- Salt and pepper to taste
- Feta cheese

Directions:
1. Tuna, olives, red onion, and hashed cucumbers should all be combined in a dish.
2. Mix the olive oil, red wine vinegar, dried oregano, salt, and pepper in a regular dish.
3. After adding the dressing, gently toss the salad.
4. Crumble some feta cheese on top.

Nutrition Information:
Kcals: 320, Protein: 30g, Fat: 18g, Carbs: 10g, Sugar: 5g, Fiber: 3g, Sodium: 700mg

23. Ratatouille with Quinoa

- Time Required : 20 mins
- Curing time: 30 mins
- Serves: 4

Ingredients:
- 1 eggplant, hashed
- 1 zucchini, hashed
- 1 yellow bell pepper, hashed
- 1 red onion, hashed
- 3 cloves garlic, hashed
- 1 can 400g hashed tomatoes
- 30ml tomato paste
- 5g dried thyme
- 5g dried rosemary
- Salt and pepper to taste
- 185g quinoa, cooked
- Fresh basil

Directions:
1. Sauté bell pepper, red onion, eggplant, zucchini, and garlic in a large pan until the vegetables are soft.
2. Add the tomato paste, salt, pepper, dried thyme, and dried rosemary along with the hashed tomatoes. Simmer for 15-20 minutes.
3. Over cooked quinoa, serve ratatouille.
4. Garnish with fresh basil before serving.

Nutrition Information: Kcals: 320, Protein: 10g, Fat: 8g, Carbs: 55g, Sugar: 12g, Fiber: 12g, Sodium: 700mg

24.   Turkey and Black Bean Chili

- Time Required : 15 mins
- Curing time: 30 mins
- Serves: 6

Ingredients:
- 500g ground turkey
- 1 onion, hashed
- 2 bell peppers, hashed
- 3 cloves garlic, hashed
- 2 cans 400g each black beans, drained and rinsed
- 1 can 400g hashed tomatoes
- 30g chili powder
- 5g cumin
- 5g paprika
- Salt and pepper to taste
- Fresh cilantro

Directions:
1. Brown ground turkey, onion, bell peppers, and garlic in a large pot.
2. Add the hashed tomatoes, chili powder, cumin, paprika, salt, and pepper, along with the black beans. Mix everything together.
3. Allow the flavors to infuse and the mixture to thicken by simmering the chili for 20 to 25 minutes.
4. Taste and adjust flavor, then serve hot with fresh cilantro on top.

Nutrition Information: Kcals: 380, Protein: 25g, Fat: 15g, Carbs: 40g, Sugar: 8g, Fiber: 12g, Sodium: 800mg

25. Caprese Salad Skewers

- Time Required : 10 mins
- Curing time: 0 mins
- Serves: 4

Ingredients:
- 1 pint cherry tomatoes
- 200g mozzarella balls
- Fresh basil leaves
- Balsamic glaze for drizzling

Directions:
1. Put fresh basil leaves, mozzarella balls, and cherry tomatoes on skewers.
2. Place the skewers in a serving platter arrangement.
3. Serve immediately with a balsamic glaze drizzled over.

Nutrition Information: Kcals: 180, Protein: 12g, Fat: 12g, Carbs: 10g, Sugar: 5g, Fiber: 2g, Sodium: 300mg

26.   Baked Cod with Mediterranean Salsa

- Time Required : 15 mins
- Curing time: 20 mins
- Serves: 2

Ingredients:
- 2 cod fillets
- 15ml olive oil
- 5g dried oregano
- Salt and pepper to taste

Mediterranean Salsa:
- 150g cherry tomatoes, 1/2 cucumber, 30g red onion, 30ml olive oil, 15ml balsamic vinegar, 15g Kalamata olives, hashed, fresh parsley

Directions:
1. Preheat oven to 200°C.
2. Coat the fillets of cod on a flat pan. Add a drizzle of olive oil and season with salt, pepper, and dried oregano.
3. Fish should be baked for 15 to 20 minutes, or until it is cooked through and flake readily.
4. Prepare the Mediterranean salsa by putting the cucumber, red onion, olive oil, balsamic vinegar, and washed cherry tomatoes in a dish and tossing them together while the cod bakes.
5. Serve the cooked cod topped with Mediterranean salsa and sprinkled with fresh parsley.

Nutrition Information: Kcals: 320, Protein: 25g, Fat: 18g, Carbs: 15g, Sugar: 5g, Fiber: 4g, Sodium: 400mg

27. Quinoa and Black Bean Burrito Dish

- Time Required : 15 mins
- Curing time: 15 mins
- Serves: 4

Ingredients:
- 185g quinoa, cooked
- 1 can 400g black beans, drained and rinsed
- 150g corn kernels
- 150g cherry tomatoes, halved
- 1 avocado, hashed
- 60g red onion, finely hashed
- Fresh cilantro
- Lime wedges for serving

Directions:
1. Combine cooked quinoa, red onion, avocado, cherry tomatoes, black beans, and corn kernels on a plate.
2. Gently toss to mix.
3. Serve with lime wedges on the side and garnish with fresh cilantro.

Nutrition Information: Kcals: 380, Protein: 15g, Fat: 15g, Carbs: 50g, Sugar: 5g, Fiber: 12g, Sodium: 600mg

28. Mediterranean Chickpea Salad

- Time Required : 10 mins
- Curing time: 0 mins
- Serves: 4

Ingredients:
- 2 cans 400g each chickpeas, drained and rinsed
- 1 cucumber, hashed
- 150g cherry tomatoes, halved
- 60g red onion, finely hashed
- 30g Kalamata olives, hashed
- 60ml olive oil
- 30ml red wine vinegar
- 5g dried oregano
- Salt and pepper to taste
- Feta cheese

Directions:
1. Combine the chickpeas, cucumber, cherry tomatoes, red onion, and Kalamata olives in a large platter.
2. Mix the olive oil, red wine vinegar, dried oregano, salt, and pepper in a regular dish.
3. After adding the dressing, gently toss the salad.
4. Before serving, sprinkle some crumbled feta cheese on top.

Nutrition Information: Kcals: 320, Protein: 15g, Fat: 18g, Carbs: 30g, Sugar: 5g, Fiber: 8g, Sodium: 800mg

29. Tomato and Basil Zoodle Salad

- Time Required : 10 mins
- Curing time: 0 mins
- Serves: 2

Ingredients:

- 2 zucchinis, spiralized into zoodles
- 150g cherry tomatoes, halved
- 60ml balsamic vinegar
- 30ml olive oil
- Fresh basil leaves
- Salt and pepper to taste
- Feta cheese optional

Directions:

1. Combine cherry tomatoes and zoodles in a bowl.
2. Whisk together olive oil and balsamic vinegar in a separate dish.
3. Over the zoodle mixture, drizzle the dressing. Toss to coat thoroughly.
4. Add freshly torn basil leaves to the salad. Add pepper and salt for seasoning.
5. If preferred, add some feta cheese as a garnish and serve.

Nutrition Information: Kcals: 160, Protein: 4g, Fat: 12g, Carbs: 12g, Sugar: 8g, Fiber: 3g, Sodium: 100mg

30.   Turkey and Vegetable Skillet

- Time Required : 15 mins
- Curing time: 20 mins
- Serves: 4

Ingredients:
- 500g ground turkey
- 15ml olive oil
- 1 onion, hashed
- 2 bell peppers, hashed
- 2 zucchinis, hashed
- 3 cloves garlic, hashed
- 5g dried Italian herbs
- Salt and pepper to taste
- Fresh parsley

Directions:
1. Brown ground turkey in olive oil in a large skillet.
2. Add the garlic, bell peppers, zucchini, and hashed onion. Sauté the veggies until they are soft.
3. Add salt, pepper, and dried Italian herbs for seasoning.
4. Before serving, garnish with fresh parsley.

Nutrition Information: Kcals: 320, Protein: 25g, Fat: 18g, Carbs: 15g, Sugar: 5g, Fiber: 4g, Sodium: 600mg

31. Grilled Shrimp and Vegetable Skewers

- Time Required : 20 mins
- Curing time: 10 mins
- Serves: 2

Ingredients:
- 200g shrimp, peeled and deveined
- 1 zucchini, hashed
- 1 red bell pepper, hashed
- 1 yellow bell pepper, hashed
- 1 red onion, hashed
- 60ml olive oil
- 30ml lemon juice
- 2 cloves garlic, hashed
- 5g dried oregano
- Salt and pepper to taste

Directions:
1. Combine olive oil, lemon juice, dried oregano, garlic, salt, and pepper on a plate.
2. Put veggies and prawns on skewers.
3. Using the olive oil mixture, brush the skewers.
4. Shrimp should be opaque after 5 minutes on either side of the grill.
5. Warm up the food.

Nutrition Information: Kcals: 280, Protein: 20g, Fat: 18g, Carbs: 15g, Sugar: 5g, Fiber: 4g, Sodium: 400mg

32. Eggplant and Red Lentil Curry

- Time Required : 15 mins
- Curing time: 25 mins
- Serves: 4

Ingredients:

- 1 huge eggplant, hashed
- 200g red lentils, rinsed
- 1 onion, hashed
- 3 cloves garlic, hashed
- 15g curry powder
- 5g cumin
- 1 can 400ml coconut milk
- 1 can 400g hashed tomatoes
- Salt and pepper to taste
- Fresh cilantro

Directions:

1. Hashed eggplant, red lentils, onion, and garlic should all be sautéed in a pot until the eggplant is tender.
2. Once fragrant, stir in the cumin and curry powder.
3. Add the hashed tomatoes and coconut milk. Cook for 20 to 25 minutes.
4. Add pepper and salt for seasoning.
5. Before serving, garnish with fresh cilantro.

Nutrition Information: Kcals: 380, Protein: 15g, Fat: 18g, Carbs: 45g, Sugar: 8g, Fiber: 15g, Sodium: 700mg

33. Turkey and Cranberry Lettuce Wraps

- Time Required : 15 mins
- Curing time: 10 mins
- Serves: 4

Ingredients:
- 500g ground turkey
- 15ml olive oil
- 1 onion, hashed
- 120ml low-sugar cranberry sauce
- 5g dried sage
- Salt and pepper to taste
- Iceberg lettuce leaves for wrapping

Directions:
1. Ground turkey should be browned in olive oil in a skillet.
2. Cook the hashed onion until it becomes tender.
3. Add dried sage, salt, pepper, and cranberry sauce and stir. Cook until well heated.
4. Spoon the turkey mixture onto iceberg lettuce leaves.
5. As wraps, serve.

Nutrition Information: Kcals: 320, Protein: 25g, Fat: 18g, Carbs: 15g, Sugar: 8g, Fiber: 2g, Sodium: 400mg

34.   Lentil and Mushroom Stuffed Bell Peppers

- Time Required : 20 mins
- Curing time: 30 mins
- Serves: 4

Ingredients:

- 4 huge bell peppers, halved and seeds removed
- 200g green lentils, cooked
- 200g mushrooms, finely hashed
- 1 onion, hashed
- 2 cloves garlic, hashed
- 5g dried thyme
- 5g dried rosemary
- Salt and pepper to taste
- 1 can 400g hashed tomatoes
- 120ml vegetable broth
- Fresh parsley

Directions:

1. Preheat oven to 180°C.
2. Sauté the garlic, onion, and mushrooms in a pan until they become tender.
3. Add the cooked lentils, salt, pepper, dried thyme, and dry rosemary and stir.
4. Put a half-cup of the lentil and mushroom mixture inside each bell pepper.
5. Combine the hashed tomatoes with the vegetable broth on a bowl. Drizzle the filled peppers with it.
6. Bake peppers for 25 to 30 minutes, or until soft.
7. Before serving, garnish with fresh parsley.

Nutrition Information: Kcals: 320, Protein: 15g, Fat: 5g, Carbs: 55g, Sugar: 12g, Fiber: 12g, Sodium: 800mg

35.   Greek Chicken and Vegetable Skillet

- Time Required : 15 mins
- Curing time: 20 mins
- Serves: 4

Ingredients:
- 500g chicken breast, hashed
- 15ml olive oil
- 1 red bell pepper, hashed
- 1 yellow bell pepper, hashed
- 1 zucchini, hashed
- 150g cherry tomatoes, halved
- 2 cloves garlic, hashed
- 5g dried oregano
- Salt and pepper to taste
- Feta cheese
- Fresh parsley

Directions:
1. Cook hashed chicken in a skillet with olive oil until it's cooked through.
2. Add red and yellow bell peppers, zucchini, cherry tomatoes, garlic, dried oregano, salt, and pepper.
3. Cook until the chicken is thoroughly covered in the seasonings and the vegetables are soft.
4. Garnish with crumbled feta cheese and fresh parsley.

Nutrition Information: Kcals: 300, Protein: 30g, Fat: 12g, Carbs: 15g, Sugar: 8g, Fiber: 5g, Sodium: 600mg

36. Cabbage and Turkey Sauté

- Time Required : 15 mins
- Curing time: 15 mins
- Serves: 4

Ingredients:
- 500g ground turkey
- 15ml olive oil
- 1 standard cabbage, shredded
- 2 carrots, julienned
- 2 cloves garlic, hashed
- 5g ground cumin
- 5g smoked paprika
- Salt and pepper to taste
- Fresh cilantro

Directions:
1. In a large skillet, brown the turkey ground in olive oil.
2. Add the chopped smokey paprika, ground cumin, shredded cabbage, julienned carrots, garlic, salt, and pepper.
3. Simmer the turkey and cabbage for a further few minutes over medium heat, tossing often, until the turkey is cooked through.
4. Make any necessary changes to the seasoning.
5. Garnish with freshly chopped cilantro just before serving.

Nutrition Information: Kcals: 320, Protein: 25g, Fat: 18g, Carbs: 20g, Sugar: 8g, Fiber: 8g, Sodium: 600mg

37. Turkey and Sweet Potato Hash

- Time Required : 20 mins
- Curing time: 20 mins
- Serves: 4

Ingredients:
- 500g ground turkey
- 2 sweet potatoes, hashed
- 1 onion, hashed
- 2 cloves garlic, hashed
- 5g ground cumin
- 5g chili powder
- Salt and pepper to taste
- Fresh parsley
- Fried eggs for serving optional

Directions:
1. In a large pan, brown the ground turkey until it is thoroughly cooked.
2. Add your preferred seasonings, hashed sweet potatoes, onion, garlic, ground cumin, and chili powder to this.
3. Simmer for long enough for the sweet potatoes to get tender and the turkey to take up the flavor.
4. If desired, serve with butter-cooked eggs on the side and top with fresh parsley.

Nutrition Information: Kcals: 350, Protein: 25g, Fat: 15g, Carbs: 35g, Sugar: 8g, Fiber: 6g, Sodium: 600mg

38.   Cauliflower and Chickpea Tacos

- Time Required : 20 mins
- Curing time: 15 mins
- Serves: 4

Ingredients:

- 1 head cauliflower, cut into florets
- 1 can 400g chickpeas, drained and rinsed
- 30ml olive oil
- 5g cumin
- 5g smoked paprika
- 2g garlic powder
- Salt and pepper to taste
- 8 standard corn tortillas
- Avocado slices
- Fresh cilantro

Directions:

1. Preheat oven to 200°C.
2. Add olive oil, cumin, smoked paprika, garlic powder, salt, and pepper to the cauliflower florets and chickpeas.
3. Bake for 15 to 20 minutes, or until the chickpeas are crispy and the cauliflower is golden.
4. Fill warm corn tortillas with the combination of roasted cauliflower and chickpeas.
5. Add some avocado slices and fresh cilantro as garnish.

Nutrition Information: Kcals: 280, Protein: 10g, Fat: 12g, Carbs: 35g, Sugar: 5g, Fiber: 10g, Sodium: 400mg

Dinner Recipes

39. Baked Salmon with Dill and Lemon

- Time Required : 10 mins
- Curing time: 15 mins
- Serves: 2

Ingredients:

- 2 salmon fillets
- 30ml olive oil
- 15g fresh dill, hashed
- 1 lemon, hashed
- Salt and pepper to taste

Directions:

1. Preheat oven to 200°C.
2. Place the salmon fillets on a flat pan in a single layer.
3. Add some fresh dill, salt, and pepper for seasoning, and then drizzle with olive oil.
4. Add the lemon slices.
5. Bake the salmon for 12 to 15 minutes, or until a fork can easily pierce it.

Nutrition Information: Kcals: 300, Protein: 25g, Fat: 20g, Carbs: 2g, Sugar: 0g, Fiber: 1g, Sodium: 150mg

40. Baked Chicken with Rosemary and Garlic

- Time Required : 10 mins
- Curing time: 25 mins
- Serves: 4

Ingredients:

- 4 boneless, skinless chicken breasts
- 30ml olive oil
- 10g fresh rosemary, hashed
- 4 cloves garlic, hashed
- Salt and pepper to taste

Directions:

1. Preheat oven to 200°C.
2. Put the chicken breasts on a baking dish to prepare them for baking.
3. Season with salt, pepper, fresh rosemary, and garlic that has been hashed. Drizzle with olive oil.
4. The chicken should be baked for 20 to 25 minutes, or until the internal temperature reaches 165 degrees.

Nutrition Information: Kcals: 280, Protein: 30g, Fat: 15g, Carbs: 1g, Sugar: 0g, Fiber: 0g, Sodium: 120mg

41. Roasted Brussels Sprouts with Balsamic Glaze

- Time Required : 10 mins
- Curing time: 20 mins
- Serves: 4

Ingredients:

- 500g Brussels sprouts, trimmed and halved
- 30ml olive oil
- 30ml balsamic glaze
- Salt and pepper to taste

Directions:

1. Preheat oven to 200°C.
2. Brussels sprouts should be seasoned with salt and pepper after being tossed in olive oil.
3. Arrange them on a baking tray in a single layer.
4. Cook for 20 minutes over high heat, or until the skin is crispy and golden brown.
5. Before serving, give it a drizzle of balsamic glaze.

Nutrition Information: Kcals: 120, Protein: 4g, Fat: 7g, Carbs: 14g, Sugar: 4g, Fiber: 5g, Sodium: 30mg

42. Spinach and Goat Cheese Stuffed Chicken Breast

- Time Required : 15 mins
- Curing time: 25 mins
- Serves: 2

Ingredients:

- 2 boneless, skinless chicken breasts
- 30g fresh spinach
- 60g goat cheese
- 15ml olive oil
- Salt and pepper to taste

Directions:

1. Preheat oven to 200°C.
2. Every chicken breast should have a butterfly on it.
3. Add pepper and salt for seasoning.
4. Add the spinach and sauté until it wilts.
5. Top each chicken breast with a layer of sautéed spinach after spreading goat cheese on one side.
6. After folding, tuck the chicken breasts in with toothpicks.
7. In a skillet that is oven-safe, heat the olive oil and sear the chicken on both sides.
8. After placing the pan in the oven, roast it for 20 to 25 minutes, or until the chicken is thoroughly cooked.

Nutrition Information: Kcals: 320, Protein: 35g, Fat: 18g, Carbs: 2g, Sugar: 0g, Fiber: 1g, Sodium: 200mg

43. Mediterranean Quinoa Dish

- Time Required : 15 mins
- Curing time: 15 mins
- Serves: 4

Ingredients:

- 185g quinoa, cooked
- 150g cherry tomatoes, halved
- 1 cucumber, hashed
- 60g Kalamata olives, hashed
- 30g red onion, finely hashed
- 75g feta cheese, crumbled
- 30ml olive oil
- 15ml red wine vinegar
- 5g dried oregano
- Salt and pepper to taste

Directions:

1. Mix the cooked quinoa, feta cheese, cherry tomatoes, cucumber, red onion, and Kalamata olives in a large bowl.
2. Mix the olive oil, red wine vinegar, dried oregano, salt, and pepper in a regular dish.
3. After adding the dressing, gently toss the quinoa mixture.
4. Allow to settle at room temperature.

Nutrition Information: Kcals: 320, Protein: 10g, Fat: 18g, Carbs: 30g, Sugar: 5g, Fiber: 8g, Sodium: 700mg

44. Cauliflower and Broccoli Gratin

- Time Required : 15 mins
- Curing time: 25 mins
- Serves: 4

Ingredients:

- 1 cauliflower, cut into florets
- 1 broccoli, cut into florets
- 30g butter
- 20g flour
- 240ml unsweetened almond milk
- 100g cheddar cheese, shredded
- Salt and pepper to taste
- Fresh parsley

Directions:

1. Preheat oven to 200°C.
2. Broccoli and cauliflower should be steamed until crisp-tender.
3. Melt butter in a pot over a medium heat.
4. Add flour and whisk until a paste forms.
5. Add almond milk gradually and mix until smooth.
6. Once the sauce thickens and the cheddar cheese has melted, stir it in.
7. Add pepper and salt for seasoning.
8. In a baking dish, mix the cheese sauce with the steamed broccoli and cauliflower.
9. Bake for 20 to 25 minutes, or until bubbling and brown.
10. Before serving, garnish with fresh parsley.

Nutrition Information: Kcals: 280, Protein: 12g, Fat: 20g, Carbs: 15g, Sugar: 4g, Fiber: 6g, Sodium: 300mg

45. Eggplant and Tomato Gratin

- Time Required : 20 mins
- Curing time: 30 mins
- Serves: 4

Ingredients:

- 2 eggplants, hashed
- 4 tomatoes, hashed
- 30ml olive oil
- 2 cloves garlic, hashed
- 5g dried thyme
- 100g Parmesan cheese, grated
- Salt and pepper to taste
- Fresh basil

Directions:

1. Preheat oven to 200°C.
2. Arrange the eggplant and tomato slices in alternating layers in a baking dish.
3. After drizzling with olive oil, add salt, pepper, dried thyme, and hashed garlic to season.
4. On top, add a little grated Parmesan cheese.
5. Bake for 25 to 30 minutes, until the vegetables are tender and the top is browned and golden.
6. Garnish with freshly chopped basil just before serving.

Nutrition Information: Kcals: 240, Protein: 8g, Fat: 15g, Carbs: 20g, Sugar: 8g, Fiber: 8g, Sodium: 400mg

46. Salmon and Asparagus Foil Pack

- Time Required : 15 mins
- Curing time: 20 mins
- Serves: 2

Ingredients:

- 2 salmon fillets
- 1 bunch asparagus, trimmed
- 30ml olive oil
- 2 cloves garlic, hashed
- Lemon slices
- Salt and pepper to taste

Directions:

1. Set the oven to 200 degrees Celsius.
2. Place a single salmon fillet on a foil-covered surface at a time.
3. Arrange the asparagus spears in a circle around the fish.
4. Drizzle with olive oil and add salt, pepper, and hashed garlic for seasoning.
5. Add the lemon slices.
6. Fold the aluminum foil into thirds to create a package.
7. Bake the salmon for fifteen to twenty minutes, or until it is cooked through.

Nutrition Information: Kcals: 320, Protein: 30g, Fat: 20g, Carbs: 8g, Sugar: 4g, Fiber: 4g, Sodium: 150mg

47. Spaghetti Squash with Tomato and Basil Sauce

- Time Required : 15 mins
- Curing time: 45 mins
- Serves: 4

Ingredients:

- 1 spaghetti squash, halved and seeds removed
- 30ml olive oil
- 2 cloves garlic, hashed
- 4 tomatoes, hashed
- 10g fresh basil, hashed
- Salt and pepper to taste
- Parmesan cheese

Directions:

1. Preheat oven to 200°C.
2. Lay down the spaghetti squash halves, cut side up, on a flat pan.
3. Add a drizzle of olive oil and season with salt, pepper, and minced garlic.
4. Roast the squash for 40–45 minutes, or until it is soft to the fork.
5. Add the fresh basil, hashed tomatoes, salt, and pepper to a pot. Simmer until the tomatoes become tender.
6. Using a fork, scrape the spaghetti squash to make "noodles."
7. Add tomato and basil sauce on top.
8. Before serving, sprinkle some Parmesan cheese on top.

Nutrition Information: Kcals: 180, Protein: 3g, Fat: 10g, Carbs: 22g, Sugar: 8g, Fiber: 4g, Sodium: 150mg

48.   Shrimp and Zucchini Noodle Stir-Fry

- Time Required : 15 mins
- Curing time: 10 mins
- Serves: 4

Ingredients:

- 500g shrimp, peeled and deveined
- 4 zucchinis, spiralized into noodles
- 30ml soy sauce
- 15ml sesame oil
- 15ml rice vinegar
- 15ml hoisin sauce
- 2 cloves garlic, hashed
- 5g ginger, grated
- Green onions
- Sesame seeds

Directions:

1. In a plate, stir together hoisin sauce, rice vinegar, toasted sesame oil, and soy sauce.
2. Heat a large pan or wok to a medium-high temperature.
3. Grate the ginger and cut the garlic for the shrimp. Cook the shrimp by stirring them until they turn pink and are well done.
4. In the wok, stir-fry the zucchini noodles for two to three minutes.
5. The sauce should be poured over the noodles and shrimp. To coat, toss in order.
6. Add some toasted sesame seeds and hashed green onions on the top of each plate before serving.

Nutrition Information: Kcals: 280, Protein: 25g, Fat: 10g, Carbs: 20g, Sugar: 10g, Fiber: 5g, Sodium: 800mg

49.   Greek Salad with Grilled Chicken

- Time Required : 15 mins
- Curing time: 15 mins
- Serves: 4

Ingredients:

- 500g chicken breast, grilled and hashed
- 1 cucumber, hashed
- 150g cherry tomatoes, halved
- 75g Kalamata olives, hashed
- 100g feta cheese, crumbled
- 30g red onion, thinly hashed
- 30ml olive oil
- 30ml red wine vinegar
- 5g dried oregano
- Salt and pepper to taste

Directions:

1. Grilled and sliced chicken breasts should be combined in a large plate with thinly sliced red onion, cherry tomatoes, feta cheese crumbles, Kalamata olives, and cucumber.
2. In a normal basin, whisk together olive oil, red wine vinegar, dried oregano, salt, and pepper.
3. Once the salad has been covered with dressing, toss it around a bit.
4. After cooking, serve right away.

Nutrition Information: Kcals: 320, Protein: 30g, Fat: 18g, Carbs: 15g, Sugar: 5g, Fiber: 3g, Sodium: 600mg

50. Baked Eggplant Parmesan

- Time Required : 20 mins
- Curing time: 30 mins
- Serves: 4

Ingredients:

- 2 huge eggplants, hashed
- 100g breadcrumbs
- 50g Parmesan cheese, grated
- 2 eggs, beaten
- 480ml marinara sauce
- 100g mozzarella cheese, shredded
- Fresh basil

Directions:

1. Preheat oven to 200°C.
2. Coat the eggplant slices in a mixture of breadcrumbs and grated Parmesan cheese after dipping them into beaten eggs.
3. The coated eggplant slices should be put on a flat pan.
4. Bake for twenty minutes, or until crisp and golden.
5. Arrange roasted eggplant pieces, shredded mozzarella cheese, and marinara sauce in a baking dish.
6. Iterate through the levels.
7. Bake for ten more minutes, or until the cheese is bubbling and melted.
8. Garnish with fresh basil before serving.

Nutrition Information: Kcals: 280, Protein: 15g, Fat: 12g, Carbs: 30g, Sugar: 10g, Fiber: 6g, Sodium: 800mg

51.   Shrimp and Quinoa Paella

- Time Required : 15 mins
- Curing time: 25 mins
- Serves: 4

Ingredients:

- 500g shrimp, peeled and deveined
- 185g quinoa, uncooked
- 1 onion, hashed
- 2 bell peppers, hashed 1 red, 1 yellow
- 3 cloves garlic, hashed
- 5g smoked paprika
- 2g saffron threads optional
- 480ml vegetable broth
- 1 can 400g hashed tomatoes
- Salt and pepper to taste
- Fresh parsley

Directions:

1. Wash the quinoa in cool water.
2. Sauté shrimp in a large skillet or paella pan until they turn pink. Take out and place aside.
3. In the same pan, sauté hashed onion, bell peppers, and hashed garlic until softened.
4. Add the saffron threads and smoked paprika and stir.
5. Add the hashed tomatoes, vegetable broth, and rinsed quinoa. Heat through to a simmer.
6. The quinoa should be cooked thoroughly after 15 to 20 minutes of cooking on low heat with a cover.
7. Add the cooked shrimp and fold in.
8. Add pepper and salt for seasoning.
9. Before serving, garnish with fresh parsley.

Nutrition Information: Kcals: 350, Protein: 25g, Fat: 10g, Carbs: 40g, Sugar: 8g, Fiber: 6g, Sodium: 800mg

52.   Tomato and Basil Zucchini Noodles

- Time Required : 10 mins
- Curing time: 5 mins
- Serves: 2

Ingredients:

- 4 zucchinis, spiralized into noodles
- 30ml olive oil
- 2 cloves garlic, hashed
- 240ml cherry tomatoes, halved
- 10g fresh basil, hashed
- 25g Parmesan cheese, grated
- Salt and pepper to taste

Directions:

1. In a large pan over medium heat, warm the olive oil.
2. Add the hashed garlic once the garlic has released its aroma through sautéing.
3. The skillet will benefit from the addition of zucchini noodles and cherry tomatoes. Simmer the vegetables for three to five minutes, or until they are crisp-tender.
4. Add some Parmesan cheese and some finely chopped basil.
5. Before serving, season with a little salt and pepper.
6. After cooking, serve right away.

Nutrition Information: Kcals: 180, Protein: 6g, Fat: 14g, Carbs: 10g, Sugar: 6g, Fiber: 3g, Sodium: 200mg

Dessert and Soup Recipes

53. Spinach and Feta Stuffed Mushrooms

- Time Required : 15 mins
- Curing time: 20 mins
- Serves: 4

Ingredients:

- 12 huge mushrooms, cleaned and stems removed
- 120g fresh spinach, hashed
- 75g feta cheese, crumbled
- 2 cloves garlic, hashed
- 30ml olive oil
- Salt and pepper to taste
- Fresh parsley

Directions:

1. Preheat oven to 180°C.
2. In a pan with a little olive oil, cook the washed spinach and garlic until the spinach has wilted.
3. Remove from the fire and stir in the crumbled feta cheese.
4. Spoon a small amount of the spinach and feta mixture into each mushroom cap's opening.
5. Place the stuffed mushrooms on a flat pan in a single layer.
6. Bake for 15 to 20 minutes, or until the mushrooms are tender.
7. Garnish with some fresh hashed parsley before serving.

Nutrition Information: Kcals: 120, Protein: 6g, Fat: 9g, Carbs: 5g, Sugar: 2g, Fiber: 2g, Sodium: 180mg

54.   Caprese Stuffed Avocado

- Time Required : 10 mins
- Curing time: 0 mins
- Serves: 2

Ingredients:

- 2 avocados, halved and pitted
- 150g cherry tomatoes, halved
- 125g fresh mozzarella balls
- Fresh basil leaves
- Balsamic glaze for drizzling
- Salt and pepper to taste

Directions:

8. To create space for the filling, cut out a little of the flesh from the center of each avocado half.
9. In the same plate, combine cherry tomatoes, fresh mozzarella balls, and fresh basil leaves.
10. Put a small amount of the caprese mixture into the cavity of each avocado half.
11. Balsamic glaze should be drizzled over the top.
12. Before serving, season with a little salt and pepper.
13. After cooking, serve right away.

Nutrition Information: Kcals: 300, Protein: 8g, Fat: 25g, Carbs: 15g, Sugar: 5g, Fiber: 10g, Sodium: 100mg

55. Berry and Yogurt Parfait

- Time Required : 10 mins
- Assembly Time: 5 mins
- Serves: 2

Ingredients:

- 240g Greek yogurt
- 150g mixed berries strawberries, blueberries, raspberries
- 50g granola
- 30ml honey
- Mint leaves

Directions:

1. In serving glasses, arrange layers of Greek yogurt, mixed berries, and granola to create a parfait.
2. Repeat the procedure of stacking.
3. Drizzle with honey over the top.
4. Garnish with few mint leaves.
5. After cooking, serve right away.

Nutrition Information: Kcals: 320, Protein: 20g, Fat: 10g, Carbs: 40g, Sugar: 20g, Fiber: 6g, Sodium: 80mg

56.   Greek Yogurt and Berry Popsicles

- Time Required : 10 mins
- Freeze Time: 4 hours
- Makes: 6 popsicles

Ingredients:

- 480g Greek yogurt
- 150g mixed berries strawberries, blueberries, raspberries
- 30ml honey
- 5ml vanilla extract

Directions:

1. In a plate, mix together Greek yogurt, mixed berries, honey, and vanilla essence.
2. Using a spoon, transfer the mixture into the popsicle molds.
3. Place popsicle sticks into each mold's center hole.
4. Place it in the freezer to solidify for a minimum of four hours.
5. Popsicles can be taken out of molds by giving them a quick rinse in warm water.
6. Enjoy!

Nutrition Information: Kcals: 120, Protein: 8g, Fat: 4g, Carbs: 15g, Sugar: 10g, Fiber: 2g, Sodium: 30mg

57.   Dark Chocolate and Berry Smoothie Dish

- Time Required : 10 mins
- Serves: 2

Ingredients:

- 2 frozen bananas
- 150g mixed berries strawberries, blueberries, raspberries
- 120ml almond milk
- 30g dark cocoa powder
- 15ml maple syrup
- Toppings: hashed strawberries, blueberries, granola, dark chocolate shavings

Directions:

1. Blend together frozen bananas, mixed berries, almond milk, dark chocolate powder, and maple syrup. Process till smooth.
2. Blend till it becomes creamy and velvety.
3. Pour the smoothie into each of the dishes.
4. Before serving, top with granola, strawberries, blueberries, and dark chocolate shavings.
5. After cooking, serve right away.

Nutrition Information: Kcals: 250, Protein: 5g, Fat: 5g, Carbs: 50g, Sugar: 30g, Fiber: 8g, Sodium: 60mg

58.   Sweet Potato and Kale Hash

- Time Required : 15 mins
- Curing time: 20 mins
- Serves: 2

Ingredients:

- 2 sweet potatoes, peeled and hashed
- 15ml olive oil
- 1 onion, hashed
- 60g kale, hashed
- 2 eggs, poached
- Salt and pepper to taste
- Paprika

Directions:

1. In a pan, warm the olive oil over a medium heat.
2. Add the sweet potatoes in dice and sauté them until they are cooked through and browned.
3. Add the hashed onion after the onion has gotten soft through sautéing.
4. Add the kale and swirl to coat, then cook until wilted.
5. Arrange a piece of the sweet potato and kale mixture onto each plate.
6. a poached egg should be placed atop each dish.
7. Before serving, season with a little salt and pepper.
8. Before serving, sprinkle some paprika over the top.

Nutrition Information: Kcals: 320, Protein: 12g, Fat: 10g, Carbs: 45g, Sugar: 10g, Fiber: 8g, Sodium: 150mg

59. Tomato and Basil Zoodle Salad

- Time Required : 10 mins
- Curing time: 0 mins
- Serves: 2

Ingredients:

- 2 zucchinis, spiralized into noodles
- 150g cherry tomatoes, halved
- 30g fresh basil, hashed
- 30ml balsamic glaze
- 15ml olive oil
- Salt and pepper to taste
- Parmesan cheese

Directions:

1. In a bowl, mix hashed fresh basil, cherry tomatoes, and zucchini noodles (zoodles).
2. Drizzle with a glaze of olive oil and balsamic vinegar.
3. To coat, toss it around a bit.
4. Before serving, season with a little salt and pepper.
5. Before serving, put some grated Parmesan cheese on top.

Nutrition Information: Kcals: 180, Protein: 5g, Fat: 10g, Carbs: 20g, Sugar: 10g, Fiber: 5g, Sodium: 150mg

60.   Almond Flour Blueberry Muffins

- Time Required : 15 mins
- Cooking time: 25 mins
- Serving: 2 muffins

Ingredients:

- 80 grams almond flour
- 45 grams fresh blueberries
- 1 huge egg
- 15 grams erythritol or another sugar substitute 2.5 grams baking powder
- 2.5 grams vanilla extract

Directions:

1. Preheat the oven to 175°C. Arrange paper liners into a muffin tray.
2. Mix the baking powder, erythritol, and almond flour in a plate.
3. In a separate bowl, beat the egg with the vanilla extract.
4. Gradually combine the dry ingredients into the wet until a batter forms.
5. Fold the blueberries in slowly.
6. Half of the batter should be placed into each liner in the prepared muffin tin.
7. A toothpick poked into the center of a muffin should come out clean after 20 to 25 mins of baking.
8. Give the muffins ten minutes to cool in the pan before moving them to a wire rack to complete cooling.

Nutritional Information: Kcals: 220 Protein: 9g Carbs: 10g Fiber: 5g Fat: 17g Sodium: 80mg

61. Strawberry Cheesecake Bites

- Time Required : 20 mins
- Freezing time: 1 hour
- Serving: 2

Ingredients:

- 4 huge strawberries
- 2 ounces cream cheese, softened
- 15 grams erythritol or another sugar substitute 2.5 grams vanilla extract
- 15 grams hashed nuts optional

Directions:

1. Using a regular spoon or knife, cut off the strawberries' tops and hollow out the insides. Put aside.
2. Mix together erythritol, vanilla essence, and softened cream cheese in a dish until well blended.
3. Each strawberry should have the cream cheese mixture inside it.
4. If desired, garnish the tops with hashed nuts.
5. Put the strawberries in the freezer for approximately one hour, or until the cream cheese has set.
6. These morsels can be eaten straight from the freezer, or you can let them come to room temperature before serving.

Nutritional Information: Kcals: 110 Protein: 2g Carbs: 5g Fiber: 1g Fat: 9g Sodium: 75mg

62. Almond Butter Cookies

- Time Required : 10 mins
- Cooking time: 12 mins
- Serving: 2

Ingredients:

- 125 grams almond flour
- 30 grams Stevia or another suitable sweetener 2.5 grams baking powder
- Pinch of salt
- 30 grams almond butter
- 5 grams coconut oil, melted
- 2.5 grams vanilla extract

Directions:

1. Preheat the oven to 175°C and line a baking sheet with parchment paper.
2. In a dish, combine the almond flour, baking soda, Stevia, and salt.
3. Mix the melted coconut oil, almond butter, and vanilla extract with the dry ingredients. Mix well enough to create a dough.
4. Separate the dough into eight equal pieces. Shape every component into a ball.
5. Place the balls on the prepared flat pan and gently press them down with the palm of your hand.
6. Bake for ten to twelve minutes, or until the edges start to become golden brown.
7. The cookies should cool on the flat pan for a few minutes after being removed from the oven, and then they should be transferred to a wire rack to cool completely.

Nutritional Information: Kcals: 210 Protein: 7g Carbs: 7g Fiber: 4g Fat: 17g Sodium: 90mg

63.   Cinnamon Roasted Almonds

- Time Required : 5 mins
- Cooking time: 15 mins
- Serving: 2

Ingredients:

- 125 grams raw almonds
- 15 grams olive oil
- 15 grams erythritol or another sugar substitute 5 grams cinnamon
- A pinch of salt

Directions:

1. Prepare a flat pan by putting parchment paper inside of it and Preheat oven to 175°C.
2. Toss the almonds with the olive oil, cinnamon, erythritol, and salt in a plate.
3. Almonds should be put out in a single layer on the flat-pan that has been prepd.
4. Bake for approximately fifteen minutes, or until the almonds are roasted and smell nutty.
5. Let the almonds come to room temperature before serving.

Nutritional Information: Kcals: 305 Protein: 10g Carbs: 12g Fiber: 7g Fat: 27g Sodium: 75mg

64. Greek Yogurt with Mixed Berries

- Time Required : 5 mins
- Serving: 2

Ingredients:

- 125 grams unsweetened Greek yogurt
- 125 grams mixed berries strawberries, raspberries, blueberries 15 grams chia seeds
- 15 grams erythritol or another sugar substitute

Directions:

1. Before serving, divide the Greek yogurt across two serving bowls.
2. Half of the mixed berries should be placed in the middle of each plate.
3. Divide the erythritol and chia seeds equally among the dishes.
4. Gobble it up right away.

Nutritional Information: Kcals: 145 Protein: 14g Carbs: 16g Fiber: 5g Fat: 4g Sodium: 40mg

65.   Sugar-Free Chocolate Avocado Mousse

- Time Required : 10 mins
- Cooling time: 1 hour
- Serving: 2

Ingredients:

- 1 ripe avocado
- 30 grams unsweetened cocoa powder
- 30 grams almond milk
- 30 grams erythritol or another sugar substitute 5 grams vanilla extract
- A pinch of salt

Directions:

1. Slice the avocado lengthwise in half to extract the pit.
2. Using a spoon, extract the avocado's flesh, then transfer it to a blender.
3. Erythritol, cocoa powder, almond milk, vanilla extract, and salt should all be combined in a blender. Process till smooth.
4. Blend until no lumps remain.
5. Before serving, let the two cups sit in the refrigerator for at least an hour after dividing the mousse between them.

Nutritional Information: Kcals: 170 Protein: 3g Carbs: 15g Fiber: 12g Fat: 15g Sodium: 75mg

Exercise and Diabetes Management

When it comes to managing diabetes, it is imperative to incorporate regular physical exercise. Regular exercise is not only something you should do because it suits you; it's also crucial for managing diabetes and improving your overall health and wellbeing. The benefits of this vital component are becoming more and more obvious as we delve further into its nuances; they go far beyond simply keeping oneself physically healthy.

Importance of Physical Activity

The significance of upholding a consistent exercise regimen for the treatment of diabetes cannot be overstated. The frequent exercise improves insulin sensitivity, which enables the body to utilize the glucose it consumes more efficiently. This in turn lowers the likelihood of insulin resistance, a problem that is common among diabetics, and helps to regulate blood sugar levels.

Furthermore, diabetes management requires maintaining a healthy weight, which can be facilitated by physical activity. Maintaining a healthy weight lowers the risk of developing diabetes-related issues, such as cardiovascular diseases, and also helps to better control blood sugar.

Since exercise acts as a catalytic component in this process, people with diabetes should focus especially on enhancing their cardiovascular health. It makes it easier to control blood pressure, promotes healthy blood circulation, and reduces the risk of heart disease—all critical components of comprehensive care for individuals with diabetes.

Tailoring Exercise to Individual Needs

Physical activity is beneficial for everyone, but the method it is approached should be tailored to the individual needs of each person. Important factors to take into account while creating an exercise program include an individual's age, level of fitness at the moment, and general health. The adage "one size fits all" does not apply to the management of diabetes; therefore, a customized approach is critical.

Individuals with diabetes ought to engage in a range of physical activities, such as strength training, flexibility training, and aerobic exercise. Walking briskly and cycling are examples of aerobic exercises that can help enhance cardiovascular health. Strength training, which results in improved insulin sensitivity and muscle function, includes resistance-based exercises. Stretching exercises, like yoga, improve flexibility and are good for one's overall health and can help with stress management, which is important for those managing the complexities of diabetes.

Overcoming Barriers to Exercise

Despite the clear benefits of regular physical activity, diabetes patients nevertheless confront hurdles that keep them from doing so. Three of the most common obstacles are lack of interest, time constraints, and hypoglycemic fear. To surmount these challenges, a multifaceted approach is necessary.

Including physical exercise into daily routines, such as opting to use the stairs instead of the elevator or taking short, rapid walks instead of lounging on the couch and watching TV, is a helpful strategy. A driving force on the path to greater physical fitness is the pursuit of social support, whether it takes the shape of workout clubs or teamwork with friends. In addition, people who have diabetes should engage closely with medical specialists to establish personalized fitness plans that are suited to their unique requirements and take into consideration any potential impediments.

Monitoring Blood Sugar Levels

A person with diabetes must closely monitor their blood sugar levels in addition to making lifestyle modifications, such as increasing their physical activity. Glycemic control can be optimally achieved when people are able to make informed decisions regarding their diet, medications, and lifestyle choices thanks to regular monitoring.

Self-Monitoring Techniques

Self-checking blood sugar levels SMBG is a cornerstone in the armament against diabetes. People can monitor their blood sugar levels at different times of the day with the help of SMBG. Modern glucometers have easy-to-use interfaces and only need a typical blood sample to give quick, precise readings.

Comprehending one's personal glycemic trends is essential for making well-informed choices. Individuals can spot patterns, identify factors that influence blood sugar levels, and promptly modify their diabetes care strategy with the help of routine monitoring.

Understanding Blood Sugar Readings

Readings of blood sugar require a deep grasp of goal ranges as well as the factors that influence glycemic management in order to effectively interpret them. Fasting blood sugar levels, which are often measured before meals first thing in the morning, reveal information about how the body responded to insulin over the previous night. The measurements taken after meals, or postprandial readings, are helpful in figuring out how different foods impact blood sugar levels.

Changes to medication, exercise regimen, or nutrition may be required if blood sugar levels stay high for an extended period of time. Conversely, hypoglycemia—a condition marked by low blood sugar—needs to be treated as away to prevent complications.

Regular Check-ups and Medical Monitoring

The most crucial component of chronic diabetes management is self-monitoring; nevertheless, regular checkups and expert medical supervision are also vital components of a comprehensive treatment plan. Experts in the medical field are crucial in assessing a person's overall health, identifying potential issues or not, and making necessary adjustments to treatment regimens.

Patients receive thorough examinations at their regularly scheduled checks, which may include blood tests that provide a detailed assessment of their metabolic condition. With the aid of these evaluations, the effectiveness of the current management plan may be assessed, and any necessary adjustments can be made.

The collaboration between individuals with diabetes and medical providers is critical. Keeping lines of communication open promotes proactive diabetes care, which helps guarantee that any new issues are addressed quickly. Consistently tracking your health is not just a reactive approach, but also a preventive one that could help you maintain optimal health and steer clear of problems.

Medications and Insulin Management

Insulin and medications play a crucial role in helping patients achieve glycemic control, even though lifestyle modifications like tracking blood sugar and engaging in physical activity are the hallmark of diabetes care. A thorough awareness of the various medication kinds available, how to deliver insulin correctly, and how to manage any potential side effects are essential for navigating the pharmaceutical landscape when treating diabetic patients.

Types of Diabetes Medications

A vast array of medications, each with a distinct mechanism of action, comprise the pharmacological toolkit for managing and treating diabetes. The liver produces less glucose and is more sensitive to insulin when metformin and similar oral medications are used. Sulfonylureas help diabetics maintain stable blood sugar levels by stimulating the pancreas to make more insulin.

Injectable medications, which increase insulin release and reduce glucagon production, such as DPP-4 inhibitors and GLP-1 receptor agonists, help improve glycemic control. SGLT2 inhibitors are a different class of oral medications that facilitate the body's more efficient excretion of glucose through the urine.

One of the mainstays of diabetes treatment is insulin, a hormone that is necessary for the metabolism of glucose. Different insulin formulations, including short-, intermediate-, and long-acting types, offer flexibility in tailoring treatment regimens to the unique needs of individual diabetes patients.

Insulin Administration and Monitoring

Giving insulin to a patient requires accuracy and adherence to prescribed regimens. Insulin pumps or subcutaneous injections are the two most common ways that insulin is given. In order to ensure proper administration and lower the risk of complications, people with diabetes must undergo the necessary training.

ongoing glucose monitoring A substantial technological advancement in the management of diabetes is provided by CGM devices. These devices allow real-time data collection on blood sugar levels and a dynamic picture of glycemic fluctuations. Because CGM devices make it simpler to make timely adjustments based on a person's responses to a variety of stimuli, such as nutrition, exercise, and other factors, they enhance insulin management.

Managing Medication Side Effects

While insulin and other medications are useful in achieving glycemic control, diabetics should still be aware of the possible side effects of these therapies. Every pharmacological category is linked to specific problems.

For example, some patients have reported experiencing gastrointestinal issues when using the medicine metformin. Sulfonylurea users must have regular blood sugar monitoring because they may have hypoglycemia. Insulin is one injectable medication that may induce injection site reactions in some patients.

As soon as possible, people should address any worries or unpleasant side effects with their healthcare providers. An open line of communication allows for the fast resolution of any prospective issues, which permits adjustments to medication schedules or the exploration of alternative alternatives.

Diabetes therapy involves more than just watching what you eat; it is a multi-step approach. Regular exercise, vigilant monitoring of blood sugar, and responsible medication management are all critical components of a comprehensive treatment plan. Individuals who have diabetes are able to confidently manage the complexity of their illness when they adopt a proactive and personalized plan. This helps these people maintain overall wellbeing in addition to glycemic management.

Conclusion

We have embarked upon a transformative exploration of nutrition, well-being, and managing diabetes through the captivating journey through the world of recipes included in the "Diabetic Cookbook." This book is an engrossing journey into the world of food. As we come to an end of this culinary trip, take some time to consider what made the most of your journey through these pages and identify the key takeaways that come through in the recipes, viewpoints, and resources that have been offered.

Using the "Diabetic Cookbook" is more than just flipping through recipes and nutritional facts; it's a deliberate choice to take back charge of your health, to overcome the constraints that are frequently related to diabetes, and to live a balanced, delicious life. The purpose of the "Diabetic Cookbook" is to empower individuals with diabetes to take back control of their health. This cookbook is your trusted companion in the field of diabetes management. In addition to recipes, it offers a philosophy—a way of living life to the fullest and enjoying meals with loved ones without compromising anything.

The book's main point, which is communicated with clarity through culinary skill and nutritional understanding, is that managing diabetes doesn't have to mean sacrificing flavor or the excitement of cooking. It's a declaration that the kitchen is a canvas rather than a battlefield and that the foods on your plate are a celebration of life as well as a source of nutrition. This statement is based on the notion that a kitchen shouldn't be a theater of war. This book is an ode to the belief that living with diabetes may be flavorful, interesting, and ultimately satisfying. Because it was written by a diabetic, it qualifies as a testament.

Whether it's breaking down the concepts of diabetic nutrition or delving into the intricacies of creating a well-balanced diabetic plate, each chapter clarifies a distinct facet of diabetes management. Together, the discussion of essential cooking tools and supplies, the subtle differences between sweeteners and substitutes, and the insights into how to administer insulin and medications provide a comprehensive guide for managing the complicated world of diabetes.

We now see exercise as a potent ally in the fight against diabetes, understanding its vital role in promoting glycemic control as well as physical well-being. We have concluded that exercise is a useful strategy for managing diabetes as a result of this. You now have a deeper awareness of the nuances of self-monitoring, the importance of routine medical checks, and the complexity of blood sugar monitoring. These newly acquired abilities will help you navigate the always shifting landscape of your health.

The original promise of a diabetic cookbook that goes beyond the ordinary has been realized: this culinary adventure has developed into a symphony of flavors, a song of nutritional wisdom, and a manual for choosing a lifestyle that is in harmony with the difficulties of diabetes. The promise has been realized, as evidenced by the variety of foods offered, which include everything from morning fare to evening specialties and are all prepared with careful consideration for both culinary appeal and nutritional balance. Not only are recipes provided, but people are also empowered to make educated decisions, understand the language of blood sugar levels, and have access to a toolkit of resources to effectively manage their diabetes.

The response that has been provided is a flexible framework that considers the distinct qualities of every single reader, as opposed to a rigid set of rules. It's an approach that recognizes the kitchen as a workspace for creativity, the plate as a work of art for nourishment, and every bite as an opportunity to savor the richness of life's experiences. This cookbook is not just a list of recipes; rather, it's an invitation to rediscover the joy of cooking, to appreciate the diverse range of flavors, and to accept the act of feeding oneself as a sign of one's dedication to taking care of oneself.

If there's one thing you learn from "The Diabetic Cookbook," make it this: You can reconsider how you relate to how food impacts your physical and emotional health. Recognize that managing your diabetes is a dynamic dance in which you take the lead and diabetes follows, rather than a static situation that needs to be maintained. Savor the many tastes life has to offer and be grateful for your freedom to create and discover new things.

Put this book aside, but let it not be the end of something; instead, let it be the start of something new: a thrilling, rewarding, and wholly personal culinary and health adventure. Beyond just a tool, the "Diabetic Cookbook" serves as a friend, a cooking instructor, and a guide towards improved health. I wish you a voyage that is as rich and satisfying as the dishes presented inside these pages. Cheers to your journey! Despite my diabetes, I extend a warm greeting to you and hope you have a life well lived.

Bonus Topic:

"The Art of Mindful Eating in Diabetes Management"

Mindful eating is an important, but often overlooked, part of the intricate treatment plan for diabetes, which involves medication, exercise, and diet. Beyond the boundaries of conventional dietary guidelines, this supplemental chapter in the "Diabetic Cookbook" invites readers to embrace a holistic perspective that extends beyond the meals on their plate.

The Essence of Mindful Eating

At its core, mindful eating is a paradigm-shifting ideology that encourages, as opposed to a restrictive diet, an intentional and deliberate connection with food. When caring for their bodies, it encourages people to savor each food, engage all of their senses, and stay present in the moment. Mindful eating can be a very useful strategy for persons navigating the challenging terrain of diabetes. It may open the door to more profound awareness of one's own wellbeing and improved blood sugar regulation.

Savoring the Present Moment

In a world where individuals often rush through meals, seeing them as little more than pit stops instead of as periods for reflection and replenishment, mindful eating offers a paradigm shift. It's an appeal to slow down, disconnect from the chaos, and savor the present moment. Individuals with diabetes will particularly benefit from this shift in viewpoint. It's an opportunity to look at mealtime as an act of self-love and self-care rather than the stress that's typically associated to it.

Breaking Free from Automatic Pilot

Mindful eaters are advised to give up the automatic way of thinking that often governs our relationships with food. It fights the tendency to eat without thinking about what, why, or how much we are eating. Making the switch from automatic to deliberate eating is essential to diabetic management. People are better equipped to make decisions that support their overall health goals and nutritional needs when they are aware of the subtle variations between hunger and fullness.

Mindful Eating and Blood Sugar Control

Over time, blood sugar control and mindful eating form a lovely partnership. Those that actively engage in their meals are more capable of making choices that will result in reduced blood sugar. Mindful eating promotes knowledge of meal composition, portion sizes, and how different meals effect blood sugar levels. This enhanced awareness, which enables more proactive and informed eating choices, is a valuable tool in the fight against diabetes.

The Pleasure Principle of Mindful Eating

Eating mindfully dispels the myth that meals appropriate for someone with diabetes have to be bland or uninspired, and instead opens the door to a world of culinary delight. It invites diners to appreciate the distinct tastes, textures, and aromas of every dish. The "Diabetic Cookbook" exhorts readers to adhere to the mindful eating philosophy, which urges individuals to value eating for genuine enjoyment in addition to providing nourishment for their bodies. This shift in perspective makes eating meals enjoyable and gratifying rather than a drudgery.

Developing Intentional Routines in the Kitchen

Mindful eating happens outside of the dining room, with the kitchen serving as the hub of the home. The "Diabetic Cookbook" bonus topic delves into the concept of mindful meal preparation. It emphasizes how important it is to be present when you chop, sauté, and combine since this is your opportunity to give each ingredient a purpose and focus. People with diabetes who cook mindfully can create a stronger connection with the act of feeding themselves as well as a sense of empowerment and creativity in the kitchen.

Handling Emotional Consumption with Awareness

This bonus topic examines emotional eating from a mindfulness viewpoint. Emotional eating is often a companion on the journey with diabetes. Mindful eating supports the identification of emotional triggers, the distinction between emotional and physical hunger, and the growth of non-food coping methods. It becomes a resilience tool, offering an alternative to bad eating behaviors for navigating the challenging emotional terrain.

Creating a Durable Bond Between Nutrition and Health

In essence, the mindful eating section of the "Diabetic Cookbook extra" is an appeal to create a meaningful and profound connection between food and wellbeing. It goes beyond food guidelines and addresses general health. Readers can learn how to better control their diabetes and investigate the basic connection between diet and lifestyle by incorporating mindfulness concepts into their culinary research. This could be a life-changing event. Meals become happy, nourishing, and empowering experiences when mindfulness is the guiding partner in the dance between the fork and the plate.

Printed in Great Britain
by Amazon